POLICE VEHICLES OF THE TWENTY-FIRST CENTURY

BRITAIN AND NORTHERN IRELAND

JOHN A. GODWIN

AMBERLEY

Authoring a publication takes considerable time, focus and persistence. I dedicate this project to my wife Karen for her steadfast support whilst I completed this book. I would additionally like to dedicate this work to my daughter Gemma, son Robert and parents John and Diana, who have accommodated my regular requests over the years to pause family journeys or make diversions so I could photograph the latest or more unusual police vehicles. I genuinely appreciate your patience.

First published 2025

Amberley Publishing
The Hill, Stroud,
Gloucestershire, GL5 4EP

www.amberley-books.com

ISBN: 978 1 3981 2647 3 (print)
ISBN: 978 1 3981 2648 0 (ebook)

British Library Cataloguing in Publication Data.
A catalogue record for this book is available from the British Library.

Typeset in 10pt on 13pt Celeste.
Typesetting by SJmagic DESIGN SERVICES, India.
Printed in Great Britain.

Appointed GPSR EU Representative:
Easy Access System Europe Oü, 16879218
Address: Mustamäe tee 50, 10621, Tallinn, Estonia
Contact Details: gpsr.requests@easproject.com, +358 40 500 3575

Contents

Author's Note

I have endeavoured to provide a broad cross-section of UK police vehicle types that were in use within the period from 2000 to 2025 from many police forces, but within the confines of a single book it has not been possible to include photographs of every force or vehicle manufacturer. Some vehicles shown were operated within this period but were delivered before 2000. The police vehicle fleets of the Channel Islands, Isle of Man and Gibraltar have been included for interest as they share many attributes with UK police forces.

All photographs included within this publication are the copyright of the author. Images have been taken on the public highway, at publicly accessible events, at specific events where police vehicle photography has been permitted, or at pre-arranged photo shoots where prior permission from the police force to take vehicle photographs has been obtained. I am grateful to the many police forces and their officers and staff who have assisted with my photographic visits over the years.

The incidental inclusion of any logos, trademarks, brand marks or similar is hereby acknowledged as being the property of their respective owners. This is not an official publication of any of the police forces or vehicle manufacturers whose vehicles are shown and has neither been approved nor endorsed by any of them.

No operationally sensitive information has been included within this publication. Information used has been collated from observing marked police vehicles at work, or from readily available public domain sources including police force and vehicle manufacturer websites, press releases and social media channels. No unmarked or covert vehicles have been included. Many of the police vehicles shown herein will already have been retired from service since they were photographed and will no longer be operational assets. E&OE.

Introduction

Within the United Kingdom, policing and law enforcement activities are undertaken by a combination of forty-five territorial police forces, each operating within a defined geographic area, three Special Police Forces (with specific jurisdictions), Ports Police (protecting ports, docks and harbours), Parks Police (covering certain parks and open spaces) and Service Police (policing within the UK Armed Forces).

One of the things they all have in common is a need for reliable transport resources, whether for general patrolling activities, the management of road traffic, controlling civil unrest or delivering a more specialist policing function. Marked police vehicles are easily identifiable by members of the public: a combination of their distinctive blue and yellow reflective markings, blue warning lights and electronic sirens leaves little doubt as to what the vehicle is. There is also a wide selection of unmarked vehicles too, used for covert operations and surveillance activities, but details of these are not included in this publication.

Within this book, we explore the many different types of police vehicles which have seen service over the last twenty-five years, since 2000, a period of many changes. Territorial police forces across the UK have given up their individual fleet liveries for the ubiquitous blue and yellow 'Battenburg' colours, we have observed the introduction of hybrid and electric police vehicles in support of environmental objectives, police vehicle resources are increasingly becoming shared between different services, and there have been significant developments in the technologies which support the use of modern emergency vehicles.

Police Vehicle Procurement

Traditionally, individual police forces will have made their own choice of vehicles without needing to follow any specific guidance. The preferred choice of supplier may have been influenced by the proximity of local vehicle manufacturing; for example, Essex Police favoured locally built Ford vehicles, Bedfordshire Police had loyalty to Vauxhall products from Luton, and West Midlands Police preferred British Leyland/Rover models from nearby Longbridge. However, in April 1986, the National Association of Police Fleet Managers (NAPFM) was formed, with the approval of the Association of Chief Police Officers (ACPO). It introduced national frameworks and procurement contracts for all UK police forces (including some non-Home Office forces and other emergency services)

Vauxhall Motors is an established provider of UK police vehicles. Three new Vauxhall Corsa cars destined for Northumbria Police have started the conversion process and await completion at one of Vauxhall's 'Special Vehicles' preparation sites in November 2009.

covering vehicles, vehicle parts, emergency equipment and vehicle disposal services. Since their introduction, these frameworks and contracts have created millions of pounds of savings for the police, and ultimately savings for the UK taxpayer.

The NAPFM works with the ACPO Vehicle Standardisation Group to standardise the use of vehicles for UK policing services. Manufacturers wishing to tender for the supply of police vehicles are required to cost vehicles using templates for each vehicle role, for example to include requirements for an auxiliary battery/split charging, second mirror, run lock functionality, calibrated speedometer, etc. The UK government's Crown Commercial Service (CCS) publishes periodic frameworks, which can be viewed online, that record the vehicle manufacturers which have been approved and can be approached with a procurement need.

At the time of writing, CCS is operating a framework agreement for the 'Purchase of Standard and Specialist Vehicles' (framework RM6244), which includes (a) 'blue light' cars and motorcycles including passenger cars, all-terrain vehicles, motorcycles, scooters and quad bikes (nineteen suppliers), and (b) 'blue light' light and medium commercial vehicles up to 7.5 tonnes (twelve suppliers). The current four-year agreement started in November 2022 and runs through to November 2026.

Police Vehicle Livery

The blue and yellow 'Battenburg' livery is the most visual identifier of a police vehicle to the public – but why is it used? The Battenburg pattern was developed in the 1990s by the Police Scientific Development Branch with four objectives: (a) to be a visible deterrent to wrongdoers, (b) to provide a visible police presence on the roads, (c) to help improve safety for police personnel and other road users and (d) to provide a conspicuous vehicle presence to protect incident scenes. Comprehensive guidance was published which addressed the implementation of the livery and the requirements for its application and use, in accordance with ACPO standards of 1998.

The police Battenburg scheme is normally applied in one of two different formats. 'Full Battenburg': two horizontal rows of alternating blue and yellow squares or rectangles, seven squares in each row, is intended for Roads Policing Units and Armed Response Vehicles for maximum conspicuity. 'Half-Battenburg': a single row of blue and yellow squares or rectangles, often with the word POLICE below, was introduced in 2004 for Basic Command Units (area commands or divisions) and Local Policing Units (local policing teams). Both versions require rear markings of red and yellow or orange and yellow chevrons.

North Wales Police CX67 AUY is a 2017 BMW 330D M Sport, demonstrating the full Battenburg livery with two horizontal bands of blue and yellow rectangles (seven in each row), with reflective markings continuing up to the vehicle's roof line.

Roof Markings

Marked police vehicles have characters applied on their roofs to help confirm their identity and role when viewed from above by police air support units or elevated CCTV camera positions in busy urban areas. Commonly applied to the roof area, some vehicles may have them fitted to their bonnet or boot panels, as available space dictates. The markings indicate three pieces of information: the police force operating the vehicle, the function of the vehicle and a unique vehicle identifier. Since 2004, thermally reflective characters have been introduced, which allow police vehicles to be identified from above during the hours of darkness using thermal cameras mounted to police helicopters.

The police force operating the vehicle is shown by a two-digit number, which relates to their Police National Computer (PNC) code, starting with 01 and 02 for London's Metropolitan Police and working through the territorial police forces to 93 for the British Transport Police, 96 for Police Scotland, 97 for the Isle of Man Constabulary and 98 for the Police Service of Northern Ireland (PSNI).

The vehicle's purpose or function is displayed by a single shape. General purpose police vehicles, including Roads Policing Units, are denoted by a circle – normally orange or black. Police dog units are identified by a black triangle, and public order vehicles by a black square. Armed response vehicles are marked with a five-pointed asterisk, with many forces also using a yellow circle at the top of the vehicle's windows to confirm its armed status to other officers on the ground. Some forces add a green cross to vehicles that are used by police medics or that are carrying comprehensive first aid equipment.

Emergency Vehicle Lighting

It is important for police vehicles to be seen when responding at speed to emergency calls, pursuing fleeing offenders or protecting an incident scene on a busy road. The UK's Road Vehicles Lighting Regulations of 1989 communicate which vehicles may display flashing lights (aside from normal direction turning indicators), and within the United Kingdom only the emergency services are permitted to display blue lights.

At the start of the period covered by this book, single spinning blue light beacons (historically known as 'Acorns') were still in use for some purposes, although the full-width lightbar was already well established by this time. Whether lightbars are fitted with individual rotating light units or the latest in integrated LED lighting technology, when activated their size makes the police vehicle highly visible from a great distance, which is important when responding to urgent incidents. Modern full-width lightbars have sufficient space for a pair of front-facing white spotlights, which can be flashing to attract attention or stationary for illumination at an incident, and a pair of rear-facing flashing red lights, which indicate that the police vehicle has stopped and provides a warning to approaching motorists. Some lightbars include message display boards.

When driven by qualified and authorised police personnel, the use of blue lights fitted to police vehicles allows the driver to make rapid progress by exempting them from observing speed limits, observing keep left and keep right signs, complying with traffic lights (including pedestrian controlled crossings) and red 'X' matrix signs on motorways, and permits them to drive in bus lanes. The driver, however, must make risk-based decisions and conduct themselves in a professional manner with full regard for the safety of other road users.

Emergency vehicles are likely to be photographed by speed cameras when responding at speed, and until recently there was a possibility that the timing of the two images recorded by the speed camera would not detect activated blue lights in between their flashing cycles. To remove that possibility, modern vehicles are now being fitted with a static blue light which is permanently illuminated when the vehicle's blue lights have been activated. When speed camera photographs are processed, this records that the vehicle was being used on an emergency call and no follow-up action should be taken.

An interesting addition to the legislation that governs the fitting and usage of blue lights to emergency vehicles also prohibits the fitting of retro-reflective blue vinyl markings to non-police vehicles. Anything that reflects blue when a light is shone onto it is treated as a blue light by the legislation, although this does not apply to non-reflective matt markings which are permissible.

Police Vehicle Life and Replacement

Individual police forces have guidelines and criteria as to how a police vehicle should be maintained and serviced, and how long it should remain operational. In the absence of a serious accident or significant mechanical failure, vehicles will be assessed using a combination of their age and mileage, as well as their ongoing suitability for police use. Vehicles that accrue a higher mileage in a shorter period, such as roads policing vehicles, will be renewed more frequently than lower mileage urban patrol vehicles or specialist vehicles. Reviewing publicly available information from several forces, the following average guidance for vehicle replacement may be in place:

- Marked response cars: 100,000 to 120,000 miles, or five years old
- Marked motorcycles: 60,000 miles or five years old
- Marked vans and carriers: 100,000 to 120,000 miles, or ten years old
- Specialist vehicles: mileage and age assessed individually

This approach sometimes presents anomalies. When West Mercia Police appointed a new fleet manager in 2013, he noted that there was a 1984 Rover SD1 still on the force's fleet list. B197 FUY had been a motorway patrol unit and driver training vehicle, but with only 106,000 miles had not yet reached the 120,000 which would have triggered its disposal. It was soon retired but now survives as a preserved classic police car.

After disposal, forces are most likely to send surplus vehicles to one of several specialist auctions across the country to receive the highest possible resale value. In the early 2000s, silver-coloured vehicles became favoured by the police as it was believed that they would provide higher resale values, although with more recent vehicles returning to a white base colour this no longer seems to be the case.

Police Driver Training

The College of Policing has specified three different levels of driver competency for police officers who are to drive police vehicles, noting that 'drive' applies equally to 'ride' for motorcycles, and that 'police vehicle' is a generic term for any vehicle used for policing purposes, whether marked or not.

Basic Police Drivers drive within the constraints of the Highway Code, are trained in stopping vehicles in normal circumstances, but do not have the authority to use emergency equipment (blue lights and sirens) to make rapid progress through traffic.

Standard Response Drivers are qualified as required by the current Police Driving Curriculum and are authorised to respond safely to incidents using response performance vehicles. They are permitted to use the vehicle's emergency equipment as circumstances require it.

Advanced Police Drivers are qualified as required by the current Police Driving Curriculum and are authorised to respond safely to incidents using advanced performance police vehicles. They are permitted to use emergency equipment as circumstances require it.

NAPFM and the College of Policing have developed an assessment that determines a police vehicle's performance using (a) its 0–60 mph acceleration time, (b) its maximum speed and (c) its bhp power rating. This formula is applied to standard response and advanced vehicles up to 3.5 tonnes in weight, electric and hybrid vehicles and motorcycles to determine the minimum driving competency level required by drivers.

Incident Response Vehicles

Local police officers will use marked cars and vans as Incident Response Vehicles (IRVs) for responding to emergency calls, routine patrols and undertaking police inquiries. These were traditionally known as 'panda cars', referring to the black police cars of decades past which had some of their body panels painted white to increase their visibility. This practice continued through the 1960s and 1970s with light blue and white coloured police patrol vehicles being commonplace.

In more recent years, examples of IRVs have included the Ford Fiesta, Ford Focus, Honda Civic, Vauxhall Astra, Vauxhall Corsa, Hyundai i30 and Peugeots 306 and 308. As basic police vehicles, the majority of IRVs will be fitted with sirens and blue lights (typically a roof-mounted lightbar) so that they can be used to respond to emergencies (subject to the driver's competency level), police communication systems and may carry traffic cones, emergency warning signs, first aid equipment and barrier tape for use at incidents and accidents. Most forces will apply half-Battenburg police markings to their IRVs.

Ford and Vauxhall dominated the police patrol car market in the early 2000s. Hertfordshire Constabulary 2000 Vauxhall Astra W733 XVS carries a single reflective stripe.

Seen in 2009, Wiltshire Constabulary 229 is a 2002 Honda Civic police patrol car, built locally at Honda's manufacturing plant in Swindon. Earlier in its police career, it carried wording for 'Special Constabulary Patrols' and 'Vehicle Sponsored by Honda'.

The Vauxhall Corsa is one of the smallest vehicles chosen to be a police patrol car. VX57 DVW is a 2007 example from West Mercia Constabulary, fitted with a mini lightbar. Its 1248-cc diesel engine produced 74 bhp and a top speed of 101 mph.

During the period covered in this book, the Ford Focus has been a popular choice as a police patrol/incident response vehicle. Hampshire Constabulary 2010 Focus TDCI HX10 ELH was noted at Brooklands Museum in Surrey in May 2011.

Several forces used the diminutive Smart ForTwo. Surrey Police's GX10 HFM was introduced in 2011 as part of the Drive SMART initiative, in partnership with Surrey County Council, and was fitted with blue lights behind the front grille.

North Wales Police use the Ford Kuga for patrolling rural areas. CX18 AUH is an all-wheel drive example, new in 2018, seen near Cefnmeiriadog in Denbighshire.

Peugeot has become a significant provider of police vehicles in recent years. FT73 CTZ is a 2023 Peugeot 3008 in the North Yorkshire Police fleet, used by their Neighbourhood Policing Teams.

Avon and Somerset Police have introduced several all-electric police patrol vehicles. KM22 PHO is a 2022 Vauxhall Corsa-e, seen near Temple Meads, Bristol, in January 2023.

Area Cars

The term 'Area Car' is used by some police forces, referring to higher performance cars positioned between IRVs and RPUs, often used by response teams when responding to the highest priority emergency calls. Area Cars are likely to be fitted with mobile data terminals and Automatic Number Plate Recognition (ANPR) technology and provide on-line data checking capabilities for police officers whilst they are out on the road. Some of the many vehicles that have been observed undertaking this role include the BMW 2 and 3-Series, Ford Focus and Mondeo, Peugeot 406, Vauxhall Insignia and Vectra, and Volvo V40 and V60.

London's Metropolitan Police has reported that their Area Cars are driven by Advanced Police Drivers, many of whom will have been trained in Tactical Pursuit and Containment (TPAC) – the safe stopping of moving vehicles. They note that Metropolitan Police Area Cars are typically deployed for:

- Pursuits of non-compliant vehicles
- Safe deflation of a non-compliant vehicle's tyres using a 'Stinger' device
- Incidents on fast roads, including road traffic collisions (RTCs)
- Locating stolen vehicles using Tracker™ technology
- Checking vehicles using ANPR

Suffolk Police 2000 Ford Mondeo ST V6 W818 JBJ, seen in September 2005.

The Metropolitan Police used Vauxhall Vectra CDX V6 cars as Borough Area Cars in the early 2000s. 2002 example LV02 HRD was seen when new in Sutton.

Seen soon after delivery in June 2022, DX22 BKE is one of the first three hybrid Volvo V60 Cross Country all-wheel drive cars to be delivered to Staffordshire Police.

Vans and Carriers

For many decades, constabularies and police forces have used the larger capacities of vans and minibuses for both general and specific policing duties. Routine uses include the rapid transport of officers to the scene of an incident, or the secure conveyance of detained persons to custody suites inside special cells within vans. The following section provides a summary of how such vehicles may be deployed.

Patrol Vehicles
Using marked police vans for general patrol purposes. This may allow the deployment of a larger number of officers within a single vehicle, or the inclusion of a prisoner cage in the rear of the van may be beneficial following the arrest of persons in remote areas, or when there would be a long delay if a dedicated prisoner transport van would need to be requested.

Officer Transport
The use of personnel carriers allows for larger groups of police officers to be driven to the scenes of incidents or events requiring a larger police presence. Such vehicles, commonly referred to as Police Support Units (PSUs), will be equipped with specialist equipment to provide protection in hostile situations, which may include a metal grille for the windscreen, toughened Perspex windows and internal door security bolts.

Transport of Detained Persons
Arrested individuals need to be securely and safely transported to custody suites in a manner that does not endanger police personnel. Specially equipped vans have one or two secure detainee cells installed in the rear of the vehicle: these are commonly equipped with lighting, ventilation, CCTV and two-way audio systems for the safety and welfare of their occupants.

Police Dogs
There is a need to rapidly deploy police dogs to the scene of incidents or crimes, and alongside estate cars, vans are converted to provide secure kennels for either one, two, four or even six dogs (in the case of the largest Mercedes-Benz Sprinters, for example). Kennel areas need to be temperature controlled, easy to clean and allow quick access to the police dogs when needed.

Specialist Functions
Vans and carriers are ideally suited due to their load space, for example carrying the extensive specialised equipment of marine and search units. They can provide purpose-built

mobile working environments for incident command units or forensics teams working for prolonged periods at the scene of a crime or major ongoing incident.

Mobile Speed Enforcement

Seen operating across the country, marked vans are commonly used for detecting the excessive use of speed and other motoring offences. Often operated by civilian Casualty Reduction Officers, they can detect speeding motorists up to a mile away on straight roads using highly accurate radar and laser guns. Many counties have formal Safety Camera Partnerships with local authorities and other public bodies, and focus their speed enforcement in areas with an unacceptable level of collisions or in response to safety concerns raised by local residents.

New in 1996 to Bedfordshire Police, long-wheelbase LDV Convoy N388 KVS was still hard at work when seen at Kempston Police Station in June 2003. This example had a 2.5-litre diesel engine.

City of London Police operated a small fleet of protected LDV Convoys for public order duties. P408 PYY, seen in Wood Street, is powered by a V8 petrol engine.

The Mercedes-Benz Sprinter has been used by UK police forces for over a quarter of a century. Kent Police 2001 example Y537 UKJ was used as a specially equipped Incident Command Vehicle, and operated for nearly twenty years until its retirement in 2020.

Sussex Police 2003 long-wheelbase Ford Transit GX53 NOU wears a distinctive yellow livery to indicate its role as a Mobile CCTV Unit. It was seen in Worthing in July 2008.

The Ford Transit can trace its policing roots back to the 1960s. This 2005 example from Lancashire Constabulary (PN05 KAA) shows the common variant fitted with a rear cell.

Hampshire Constabulary has used many Volkswagen Transporter vans over the years for enforcing speed limits and detecting other road traffic offences. HX56 VJZ is a 2006 example.

Police Scotland was formed in April 2013, bringing together the eight existing regional police forces of Scotland, one of which was Dumfries and Galloway Constabulary. Seen at the since closed Gretna Green police station in February 2009 is Vauxhall Vivaro 2900 SJ56 HBG, which had been new in 2006.

Seen when new in May 2007, Lincolnshire Police Mercedes-Benz Sprinter FX07 JHZ is equipped as an Operational Support Unit. Note the windscreen grille, headlight protectors and toughened side windows.

A later Mercedes-Benz Sprinter model is seen in use with West Yorkshire Police; YJ66 BJU is standing by in Leeds City Centre in July 2019. Note the absence of a conventional lightbar, with blue lights having been installed high on the vehicle's sides instead.

Seen in Oban in September 2020, Police Scotland SF68 ARU is a 2018 diesel-powered Ford Transit Mark 8, used for local patrols and the transport of arrested persons to custody.

Roads Policing Units

Traffic Officers assigned to a police force's Roads Policing Unit (RPU) provide high visibility roaming police patrols across the motorway and main trunk road network of each territorial police force area. The Roads Policing Strategy of the National Police Chief's Council's 'Policing Our Roads Together' sets out five areas of focus:

- The reduction of casualties on the roads
- Counter-terrorism activities
- Reducing the anti-social use of roads
- Denying criminals use of roads and
- Public reassurance by high visibility patrols of the road network

RPUs are commonly tasked to respond to serious RTCs on fast roads, which may involve putting road closures in place, interviewing drivers and witnesses, and the management of traffic backlogs. RPU officers are required to be Advanced Police Drivers and trained in traffic law, including a detailed knowledge of the regulations for large goods vehicles (LGV), passenger carrying vehicles (PCV) and the transporting of dangerous loads.

RPU vehicles are similarly equipped to Area Cars, although they will carry additional emergency signage, traffic cones and equipment to preserve evidence at the scenes of an incident. This may involve the taking of measurements and creating plans of vehicle positions, the obtaining of scene photographs and recording detailed evidence for use in any subsequent investigations. A specific Collision Investigation Unit (CIU), part of the RPU, uses specially trained investigators to fully understand the circumstances of an incident: an important assessment for supporting any criminal prosecutions that may follow.

At the turn of the twenty-first century, RPUs were using high-performance vehicles such as Vauxhall Senators and 2.5- and 3.0-litre Vauxhall Omegas, the Land Rover Discovery, Range Rover, Volvo V70 and BMW 530 series. Many forces favoured the estate version of these marques, the larger load area being ideal for the volume of additional equipment which needed to be carried. Their larger capacity engines were suited to carrying the additional weight, as well as providing an emergency towing capability for rescuing stranded vehicles. In more recent times, most territorial police forces have drawn vehicles for road policing from a similar set of manufacturers, including BMW (330, 530 and X5), Volvo (V60, V90, XC70 and XC90), Audi (A4 and A6), Mitsubishi Shogun, Skoda Octavia VRS and Volkswagen Touareg. The BMW R1200RT motorcycle is a popular choice for roads policing purposes.

Until recently, BMW had a significant share of the market for vehicles used by RPUs. Following the tragic death of a Cumbria Police RPU officer in 2020, in an accident later attributed to a fault with BMW's N57 straight-six diesel engine, it was investigated and identified that the cause was the unique way in which BMW police vehicles were being used. BMW, noting that similar issues had not been experienced with non-police vehicles, advised police forces to upgrade the oil being used and to reduce oil change periods to no more than every 10,000 miles. However, several other forces had reported vehicle fires and chose to either reduce or end their dependency on BMW cars, and in January 2023, BMW announced that it would no longer be selling its cars to UK police forces. Volvo, as an alternative supplier of performance vehicles suitable for roads policing duties, has increased its market share as a result.

Roads Policing Unit Equipment

To support their specialist role, RPU vehicles are fitted with various systems and equipment which allow them to monitor and record the activities of other road users. These include:

ProVida is an in-car video recording system that is fitted to both police cars and motorcycles and includes full-colour pan and zoom cameras in both the front and rear of the police vehicle, as well as a capability to record footage alongside supporting date, time and speed data. The latter is achieved using an in-built VASCAR system (see below) which records the speeds of road users either in front or behind the observing police vehicle. Colour monitors are also installed for RPU officers' use. The recordings can be used as evidence in a court of law.

VASCAR (Visual Average Speed Computer and Recorder) allows RPU officers to determine the speed of a moving vehicle, whilst they are in motion themselves. Invented in 1966 and introduced into service in the early 1970s, VASCAR units are normally mounted on the police vehicle's dashboard, with an odometer unit connected to the police vehicle's transmission. White lines, squares or circles painted on the road surface are a set distance apart and are used to time a vehicle's speed between two fixed points.

ANPR (Automatic Number Plate Recognition) uses a combination of high-resolution colour and infrared camera systems to record the registration plates of vehicles which pass by a police vehicle. Each number plate is instantly checked against police databases, providing near real-time notifications of stolen vehicles, wanted persons, uninsured drivers, expired MOTs and untaxed vehicles.

Tracker™ is a vehicle tracking system that is fitted to more than 2,000 UK police vehicles, all NPAS police helicopters and at major seaports. Vehicles fitted with a Tracker system can be tracked by the police to within 1 metre if stolen, including within shipping containers or underground car parks using VHF frequencies. Tracker's website notes that more than 28,000 stolen vehicles with a value of nearly £600 million have been recovered using the firm's technology and partnership with UK police forces.

Calibrated speedometers are required to ensure accurate speed readings which can be used as evidence. Both traditional and electronic speedometers can be calibrated by a specialist company that has ISO 17025 accreditation, the international standard for testing and calibration laboratories.

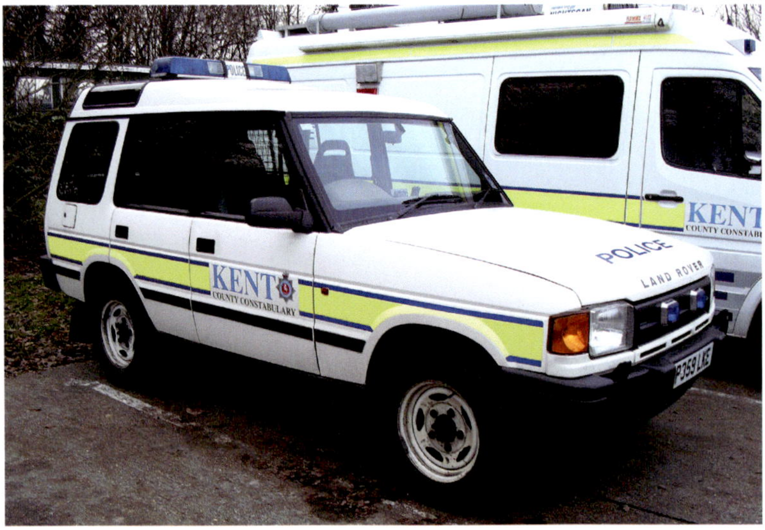

In use with Kent County Constabulary's Roads Policing Unit in December 2003 was P359 LKE, a 1997 Land Rover Discovery TDI. It was photographed at their Aylesford Traffic Base.

At the start of the 2000s, the Vauxhall Omega in both saloon and estate form was the most popular choice for Roads Policing Units. Hertfordshire Constabulary KC02 KCJ is a 2002 V6 example that was photographed at their Hitchin Traffic Base in July 2003.

Thames Valley Police 2002 Vauxhall Omega V6 OV02 YKH was photographed when new. It is an example of the saloon variant of the Omega and carries Thames Valley Police's 'jam sandwich' colour scheme with a single orange stripe.

Essex Police operated a fleet of high-performance Ford Mondeo ST220 traffic units. EY53 FRP has a top speed of 155 mph, and a 0–60 time of 7.6 seconds through its six-speed gearbox.

This June 2005 photograph shows Gwent Police Volvo V70 T5 CN04 GRU leaving the former Cwmbran Headquarters. Note the additional nearside mirror fitted for the passenger's use.

Cheshire Police patrol the M6 motorway from their base at Knutsford Services. 2004 Range Rover Vogue DK04 GHN is powered by a 4.4-litre V8 petrol engine.

Sussex Police Roads Policing Unit BMW 530D M Sport Touring GX07 FUD, seen when new in 2007 in Burgess Hill. Note the ANPR camera fitted to the roof of the car.

In October 2008, Mitsubishi Motors introduced a police specification version of the Lancer Evolution X. Essex Police, Humberside Police and South Yorkshire Police all used them operationally for roads policing, with their 295 bhp powering from 0–60 mph in a little over five seconds.

The BMW 5-Series has been a popular choice for Roads Policing Units. Kent Police operated a fleet of BMW 530D cars, including GN62 EWY, seen near Maidstone.

Warwickshire Police 2020 Volvo XC60 AWD (all-wheel drive) KS70 OBX is a traffic car within the force's Operational Patrol Unit. It is operated by Special Constabulary Roads Policing volunteers.

This 2001 Ford Galaxy Ghia 24V was used by Sussex Police for Crash Investigation assignments. Y314 GFG was photographed at Shoreham Airport in May 2004.

Hampshire Constabulary used long-wheelbase Mercedes-Benz Sprinter HX56 AWF as a Roads Policing Incident Support Unit. It carried a large quantity of emergency equipment.

Armed Response Vehicles

UK police forces deploy Armed Response Vehicles (ARV) to incidents involving the use of firearms, where there is a suspected involvement of weapons or to other high-risk situations where an armed response by the police may be called upon. ARVs were first used in the UK by the Metropolitan Police in London in 1991. Most UK territorial police forces are routinely unarmed and call upon their roaming ARVs as the circumstances of an incident dictate. Only three UK police forces routinely arm their operational officers to counter the risks associated with their specific activities – these being the Ministry of Defence Police, the Civil Nuclear Constabulary and the Police Service of Northern Ireland.

With ARVs needing to combine high-performance capabilities with a large load carrying capacity, at the start of this century ARVs used similar performance vehicles to RPUs, including Vauxhall Omegas, Volvo V70s and the BMW 5-Series. More recently, favoured ARV models selected by UK police forces have included the Audi Q7, BMW X5, Mitsubishi Shogun and Volvo XC90. Marked ARVs are identifiable either by a fluorescent yellow five-pointed asterisk displayed at the top of the windows front and rear, or in London by a fluorescent yellow circle. Regardless of the police force, all ARVs have an asterisk displayed on the roof, to enable rapid identification of their role by police air support units flying above.

Following the 2011 civil disturbances across the UK, Avon and Somerset Police approached OVIK Solutions of Dorset to repurpose former British Army 'Snatch' Land Rover Defenders for police use. The OVIK 'Phoenix' vehicles were required to undertake firearms and public order duties, having ballistic protection and other defensive controls including window grilles and ground skirts fitted to protect the underside.

ARVs are operated by Authorised Firearms Officers (AFOs) or Specialist Firearms Officers (SFOs) with specially modified vehicles suited to this task. They will be prepared so that their performance and handling are not adversely impacted by the additional weight associated with the ARV's officers and their equipment. ARVs are fitted with secure safes within which handguns, rifles, baton guns and other weapons and ammunition can be securely stored. SFOs receive additional training on tactics for dynamic entry and hostage rescues.

In 2005, the Heckler & Koch baton gun was introduced, which fires an attenuating energy projectile in circumstances when incapacitation is required without the use of conventional weapons. In 2007, the Home Office approved the introduction of less lethal Tasers (manufactured by Axon), which provide a further non-lethal incapacitation option by the delivery of a 1,500-volt charge to the body by a modulated electric current, designed to cause involuntary muscle contractions. More recently, Tasers have started to be deployed to other police units that would not normally be armed, for example, Police Support Units.

K414 SHR is a 1993 Land Rover Defender V8, which started life with the Ministry of Defence as a 'Snatch' armoured vehicle. Updated and converted by OVIK Solutions to become the OVIK 'Phoenix', this demonstrator later joined the Avon and Somerset Police fleet.

New to Bedfordshire Police back in 2000, X793 MBM was a Ford Galaxy Ghia 24V, in use as an Armed Response Vehicle. Note the blue star on the bumper and the blue lights in the door mirrors.

In the early 2000s, the City of London Police's Tactical Firearms Group used FP51 OLR, a 2001 Mercedes-Benz E320 CDI. This vehicle type was not widely used by UK police forces.

Surrey Police used Audi Q7 Quattro police demonstrator OY59 MWC as an ARV in January 2010, a capable vehicle for the snow and ice that were covering the Guildford area at the time.

Seen when new in 2010 at Hullavington Airfield, Wiltshire Police BMW X5 3.0D WX10 HOA (204) was one of the force's Armed Response Vehicles.

The performance and load-carrying ability of the BMW X5 made it an ideal Armed Response Vehicle. This 2018 example is part of the Hampshire Constabulary and Thames Valley Police Joint Operations Unit. OU18 AYW is seen near Milton Keynes when new.

Armed Response Vehicles (Airports)

Territorial police forces will deploy ARVs if their operational area includes a significant airport: the Metropolitan Police protects Heathrow Airport, Sussex Police covers Gatwick Airport, Bedfordshire Police serves Luton Airport and Essex Police has responsibility for Stansted Airport, for example. Due to the nature of potential threats and incidents at international airports, it is common for specially protected vehicles to be routinely allocated to airport police fleets. Such ARVs may include the installation of ballistic/bulletproof protection to windows and doors of standard vehicles such as the Range Rover, through to the complete design and production of customised vehicles to meet a police force's bespoke specifications.

In July 2002, London's Metropolitan Police took delivery of a trio of armoured Chevrolet 3500 trucks, fitted with heavily armoured bodies which had been manufactured by Jankel Armouring Ltd of Surrey. Their large size, powerful Chevrolet engines and distinctive dark blue colour made them stand out as vehicles which had enhanced capabilities: all three were put to work at Heathrow Airport in readiness for serious incidents, including the increased possibility of further terrorist attacks after the tragic events of 11 September 2001.

Following several years' assessment of their capability, the Metropolitan Police proceeded to order a batch of larger Jankel Guardian bodied Ford F-450 Super Duty 4×4 vehicles. Some of these were allocated to Heathrow and London City Airports, whilst others were equipped to respond to the most serious firearms and public order incidents within the wider London area. Several Jankel Guardians were also ordered by Essex Police, the only examples to be used outside of the Capital. Whilst the detailed security specification has not been disclosed, Jankel publicity materials indicated that each vehicle:

- Weighs in at just under 7,000 kg, and can carry up to eight officers and their equipment
- Is a 4×4, powered by a 6-litre, V8 turbo diesel engine, producing 325 bhp
- Has two doors to the front cab, rear doors and a kerbside door
- Is resistant to public order threats, petrol bombs and 7.62 calibre bullets
- Has run flat tyres, using the Hutchinson VFI system
- Is fitted with protective bars to the front, with options for other specialist equipment as required

2005 Metropolitan Police Ford F-450 Super Duty 4x4 with a V8 turbo diesel engine and armoured Jankel Guardian bodywork, one of several allocated to London's Heathrow Airport.

Greater Manchester Police MX04 UWG is an armoured 2004 Range Rover TD6, used to patrol the perimeter areas surrounding Manchester Airport. Note the amber rooflights, 'ARV' red square, and the thickness of the protected window surrounds.

Sussex Police has responsibility for protecting Gatwick Airport, near Crawley. Previously having served with the British Army, R502 LDE is an armoured Land Rover Defender CAV 100 ARV. It is seen at the airport in June 2006.

Seen at Birmingham Airport in May 2004 is Land Rover 110 F809 DOE from 1989, one of several armoured vehicles deployed by West Midlands Police to protect the airport.

Parliamentary and Diplomatic Protection Vehicles

Some of the most distinctive Armed Response Vehicles in the UK are operated by the Metropolitan Police's Parliamentary and Diplomatic Protection (PaDP) branch, being bright red in colour.

Originally formed as the Diplomatic Protection Group (also known as SO16) in 1974, its original purpose included the protection of diplomatic establishments such as embassies in Central London, as well as providing support for state visits, royal events and similar high-profile activities. A further Metropolitan Police branch was the Palace of Westminster Division (SO17), responsible for the security of the UK parliamentary estate in London. In April 2015, SO16 and SO17 merged to form the PaDP, which became the largest armed police unit in the country.

Back in the early days of the DPG, an Austin 1800 and Hillman Hunter were selected to receive a new red livery, with red being chosen for its association with royalty and diplomacy. The reason for the colour was to assist the diplomatic community with quickly identifying the police personnel responsible for their safety. Whilst there was a move in the early 2000s to replace red with silver vehicles, the DPG successfully challenged that the red scheme had worked well over the previous twenty-five years and should be allowed to continue.

In more recent years, PaDP has used red BMW X5s, Ford Transits, Mercedes-Benz Sprinters and Vauxhall Vivaro vehicles, many of which carry the fluorescent yellow circle denoting their armed status.

At the start of the 2000s, the Metropolitan Police's Diplomatic Protection Group introduced a fleet of Vauxhall Zafira cars. LX03 NYW, a 2003 automatic example, demonstrates the DPG's distinctive red-based scheme in this July 2005 photograph.

Amongst more recent deliveries to the Metropolitan Police's PaDP fleet are Ford Transit Custom 340 carriers, powered by Ford's 2.0-litre EcoBlue diesel engine. BX22 AVJ is seen opposite the Houses of Parliament in March 2024.

Northern Ireland – Tangis and Pangolins

The armoured Land Rover Tangi was designed for use by the Royal Ulster Constabulary (RUC) during the Troubles in Northern Ireland. Armoured vehicles were introduced in the late 1950s with basic protection applied to the Land Rover 109 with a metal cage fitted over the pickup bed; ballistic protection was later added to provide protection against firearms. The Land Rover 'Hotspur' followed in the late 1970s, again using the Land Rover 109 but now fitted with armour-plated bodywork and bulletproof glass. Later developments for the Hotspur included the fitment of polycarbonate body panels and the addition of rubber skirts and grilles to ground level to prevent attacks to the underside of the vehicle.

With the Hotspurs needing to be replaced, the 'Simba' was intended to be the new model for the RUC, incorporating an advanced armoured body to the Land Rover. Unfortunately, delivery was slow, so attention switched to the Land Rover Tangi, the first of which entered service in early 1986. These comprised the armour from current Hotspurs being fitted to conventional Land Rover Defender chassis, retaining the skirt protection and fire extinguishing system, and gaining steel radiator protection, a spotlight and blue lights to the front and rear of the roof. A second ballistic steel roof was fitted to provide protection from bombs landing on top of the vehicle. Production of new Tangis and upgrades to the existing fleet continued into the early 1990s.

The RUC became the Police Service of Northern Ireland in November 2001, and during the intervening years the operational Tangi fleet has been reduced significantly. A 2021 Freedom of Information Act request confirmed only four Tangis remained operational, with 106 in the reserve fleet. Some Tangis were sold on to UK mainland forces such as South Yorkshire Police and West Yorkshire Police for continued use as armoured vehicles

The PSNI's next armoured vehicle was introduced in 2011. OVIK's Pangolin Armoured Personnel Carrier (APC) was based on a Land Rover 110 or 130 chassis, powered by a 2.4-litre Puma diesel engine, with uprated braking and suspension. Armoured panels, fire suppressant systems, fireproofing of the fuel tank, fire resistant paint, run-flat tyres and surveillance systems all contributed to the safety and security of the vehicle's occupants.

Displayed at the NAPFM Event in Wiltshire in August 2003, PSNI Land Rover Tangi DAZ 5796 demonstrates the resilience required from armoured patrol vehicles in Northern Ireland.

Also at the annual NAPFM Event, this time in 2011, was a new and unregistered PSNI Land Rover Pangolin which had yet to enter service, and was being displayed by manufacturer OVIK Solutions.

Water Cannons

Whilst used across the globe, the police water cannon has only six operational examples within the whole of the United Kingdom, all of which belong to the Police Service of Northern Ireland (PSNI). The PSNI had requested water cannons as a less-lethal replacement for the use of baton rounds, and a review by the UK's Defence Scientific Advisory Council of the MOL MSB18 water cannon in use with the Belgian Federal Police followed. This resulted in an order for six Dutch GINAF chassis with permanent six-wheel

Whilst not a UK police vehicle, this Belgian Federal Police MOL MSB18 water cannon seen in Brussels was the type assessed before the PSNI was authorised to place an order for six of their own.

drive, paired with Somati RCV9000 water cannon equipment, with the first two arriving in August 2003. Each unit operates with a crew of four police officers.

PSNI water cannons are only authorised for use within Northern Ireland, and not elsewhere within the UK. In November 2023, following civil disturbances in Dublin, Ireland's An Garda Síochána requested to borrow PSNI water cannons under a mutual aid agreement. Two of the six were promptly sent south, but they were only to be operated by Garda and not PSNI officers. They both received local Irish vehicle registrations from Dublin.

London's Metropolitan Police was authorised to acquire a trio of second-hand Ziegler Wasserwerfer 9000 water cannons from Germany's Bundespolizei (Federal Police) in 2014. Prior to delivery to London, these were overhauled with a black paint scheme with a single line of Battenburg livery applied and fitted with updated CCTV and monitoring systems. They remained as left-hand drive, and to conceal their age, dateless plates from Northern Ireland were fitted. In 2015, the then Home Secretary declined to approve their operational use, following a review of their safety and effectiveness, so they stayed in store at a secure location until being scrapped in 2018, having never been used in service by the Metropolitan Police.

Police Service of Northern Ireland water cannon 005 (XCZ 4924), a 2004 GINAF permanent six-wheel drive chassis fitted with Somati's RCV9000 water cannon system.

Mounted Section Horseboxes

At the time of writing, there are thirteen UK territorial police forces operating police horses within their respective mounted sections. These are Avon and Somerset Constabulary, the City of London Police, Gloucestershire Constabulary, Greater Manchester Police, Lancashire Constabulary, Merseyside Police, Metropolitan Police, Northumbria Police, Police Scotland, South Wales Police, South Yorkshire Police, Thames Valley Police and West Yorkshire Police. Of these, the Metropolitan Police is the largest, with approximately 100 horses and 125 full-time personnel. A further five established mounted sections were discontinued during the period covered by this book: West Midlands Police (1999), Royal Parks Constabulary (2004), Essex Police (2012), Nottinghamshire Police (2012) and Cleveland Police (2014).

Police horses are often deployed on high-profile policing tasks, including neighbourhood policing. They are acknowledged as being a visible deterrent in preventing crime, and their presence provides reassurance to the communities within which they work. They are often seen at large-scale public order events and assisting with crowd control at busy football stadiums. With only a small number of UK police forces having this useful resource, mounted sections are frequently assigned to assist other police forces at specific events.

With a clear need to be able to safely and securely transport police horses to where they are needed, mounted sections operate horse transporters. These are typically based

The Royal Parks Constabulary operated a Mounted Branch until its abolition in 2004. Seen in Richmond Park in 2002 is their 1985 Ford horsebox C547 ORX.

on a lorry chassis with a custom-built horsebox from specialist providers such as the KPH Helios and Oakley Supreme, weighing between 7.5 and 26 tonnes, and which can transport between two and six horses. Whilst these lorries will carry police livery, they are not response vehicles and therefore are unlikely to be fitted with blue lights or sirens.

Police forces need to follow DEFRA guidance which specifies how long police horses can be transported for, and they will be fitted with protective boots, knee protectors and tail bandages to prevent injury during their journeys. Equipped with hay feeders, drinking water (when stationary), anti-slip floor coverings, CCTV observation systems and air conditioning, personnel travel with horses in transit so that they are not left unattended at any point.

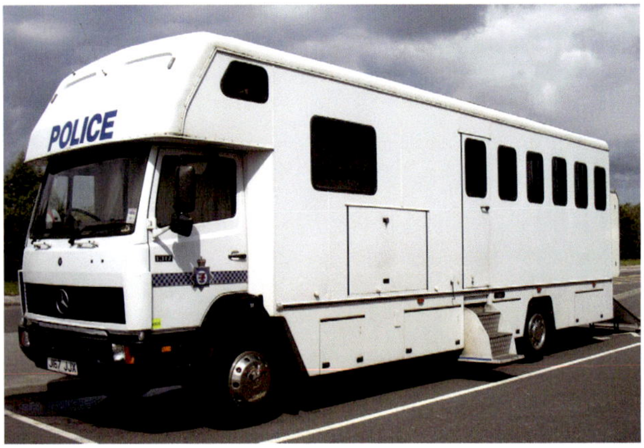

Left: Seen in July 2004 at their Portishead HQ, Avon and Somerset Constabulary were operating this large but minimal-liveried Mercedes-Benz 1317 horsebox, J167 JJX.

Below: Observed in Royal Windsor in September 2009 is Thames Valley Police's 2004 Mercedes-Benz Atego 'Olympic IV' OU04 FZC, used by the force's Mounted Section who were patrolling nearby.

City of London Police 2005 Scania P270/Oakley Supreme LY05 KNE.

Cleveland Police's Mounted Section was wound down in 2014 as a cost-saving measure. Their 2010 Iveco Eurocargo NX10 FGP was then passed to Northumbria Police for further use.

Police Lorries

In previous chapters, we have observed how larger lorries are used by police forces for transporting police horses and as the basis for water cannons in Northern Ireland. Expanding upon these specific uses, many UK police forces use lorries for other specialist policing purposes, for example as mobile police stations, incident command units, search units and forensic units. The Metropolitan Police in London also operates a fleet of

In 2006, Lincolnshire Police were using Iveco L677ECX as an Underwater Search Unit.

Surrey Police operated several Iveco Mobile Police Stations by 2005, equipped with cells, interview rooms and toilets. N505 YOF, seen here, later served in the Cheshire Police fleet.

marked vehicle removal lorries which are used for transporting seized vehicles or parking enforcement in areas such as Heathrow Airport. Commonly based on commercial chassis provided by DAF, Ford, Iveco, Mercedes-Benz, Renault, Scania and Volvo, some examples of their many different policing roles are shown in this section.

Above left: Avon and Somerset Constabulary Mercedes-Benz 1820L R302 DEU was used as a Command Unit when seen at their Portishead HQ in July 2004. It later received Battenburg colours.

Above right: Thames Valley Police 2003 Mercedes-Benz Atego OV03 LHW was used as a mobile Forensic Investigation Unit.

New in 2007 is Merseyside Police's Mitsubishi Fuso Canter two-car transporter, completed by Roger Dyson Recovery Systems of Droitwich, Worcestershire. Primarily used for police vehicle recovery, it carries Battenburg livery and has been fitted with blue lights.

Police Dog Section Vehicles

Almost all UK police forces operate police dogs in support of both generic and specific policing activities. The first recorded use of police dogs dates back to 1888, when Metropolitan Police Commissioner Charles Warren tested two bloodhounds in the hunt for Jack the Ripper. The trial failed: one dog bit the Commissioner and then they both ran away. In 1907, the North Eastern Railway Police were impressed by police dogs being used in Belgium, and Inspector Dobson created the first police dog section using four Airedale Terriers which were deployed at Hull Docks in 1908.

The North Eastern Railway Police later became part of the British Transport Commission Police, which at the time used twenty-four police dogs. Today known as the British Transport Police (BTP), their dog section celebrated its centenary in 2007, at which point over sixty operational police dogs were on the force – one of the largest police dog sections in the country. Across the UK, police dogs comprise:

- General service dogs, for crowd control, tracking of suspects, location of victims and similar duties
- Explosive detection dogs, trained to identify and locate explosive materials
- Drug detection dogs, trained as Passive Alert Detection (PAD) dogs, to signal the location of drugs
- Cash/weapons dogs, focused on locating large quantities of cash or firearms

Peugeot Expert vans were a popular choice for dog units at the turn of the century. Sussex Police operated several; S406 CFG is a 1988 1.9 turbo diesel example, seen in Horsham.

With the timely deployment of police dogs in support of policing activities being of utmost importance, the requirement for police dog vehicles combines the need for performance with maintaining the safety and welfare of the valuable dogs being carried. This typically includes:

- Warning lights, sirens and secure radio systems
- Secure dog kennels, for either one, two, four or six dogs, depending upon vehicle size
- Climate or temperature-controlled kennels, to ensure police dogs remain comfortable in all weathers
- Kennels lined with fibreglass for ease of cleaning
- Marked vehicles being identified by a black triangle as part of their roof markings

Right: Thames Valley Police Dog Section's 1999 Ford Escort 55 V606 RUD was photographed at Abingdon Police Station in Oxfordshire in September 2002.

Below: The British Transport Police operated two six-kennel Mercedes-Benz Sprinters from its Dog Training School in Tadworth, Surrey. Y394 HGX and Y395 HGX were fitted with windscreen grilles and other protective features, as they were available to be deployed on operational tasks.

The estate version of the Ford Focus was a popular dog unit vehicle for many forces. Leicestershire Police FG52 VAF, new in 2003, was photographed near Peterborough.

Wandsworth Parks Police transported their police dogs in a pair of 2008 Ford Transit Connect TDCI vans. EJ08 KKV was seen in March 2010 by the Peace Pagoda in London's Battersea Park.

The Vauxhall Zafira was a popular choice for dog sections in the 2010s. Thames Valley Police 2010 example OU60 ENO includes wording that 'This Vehicle is Air Conditioned for Animal Welfare' and has a black triangle roof marking.

Seen when new, 2019 Ford Mondeo Estate YX19 DCE is used by Humberside Police's Dog Section. Its size is ideal for carrying two kennels within the rear of the vehicle.

Surrey Police and Sussex Police have merged their Police Dog Units into a single resource, hence both crests are featured on the door of this 2020 Skoda Superb, seen near Farnborough in Hampshire.

Rural Policing Units

An increasing number of police forces have implemented teams specifically focused on the identification and investigation of rural crimes. Their remit includes agricultural crime (theft of machinery or from farm buildings), equine crime (tack theft or livestock worrying), wildlife crime (poaching, hare coursing and interfering with protected species) and heritage crime (damage to ancient monuments, theft of lead from church roofs, etc.), as well as implementing crime prevention initiatives in each of these areas. For reliable

Lincolnshire Police 2001 Land Rover Discovery X523 JUK was being used as a Wildlife Crime Officer vehicle in May 2007, often seen on patrol across the county's wide rural areas.

transport into remote rural communities, and to police off-road environments, 4×4 vehicles such as the Ford Ranger, Isuzu D-Max, Land Rover Freelander, Defender and Discovery and Toyota Hilux are amongst those commonly used. Some forces have added quad bikes and ATVs (all-terrain vehicles) to their fleets for their enhanced off-road capabilities.

Humberside Police's Rural Task Force used 2016 Isuzu D-Max YY16 XXH for its Wildlife and Rural Crime Officer. It has a 2.5-litre turbo diesel engine paired with a six-speed manual gearbox.

Avon and Somerset Police use Ford Rangers for their Rural Affairs Unit. 2021 example EN21 XTC was noted at the Bath and West Showground at Shepton Mallet in June 2024 with officers providing crime prevention advice to residents of rural communities and local farmers.

Police Motorcycles

A long-established part of the police fleet has been the motorcycle. Their small size allows them to make good progress through heavy traffic, and their performance makes motorcycles valuable assets for roads policing, as well as providing escort services for parades, security convoys and public events. Modern marked motorcycles are liveried with the reflective Battenburg scheme, have blue lights and sirens, a police radio and possibly cameras and speed monitoring equipment.

Sussex Police Honda Pan European ST1100 X186 VUF, seen in Worthing in July 2010. Already ten years old, this motorcycle would soon be withdrawn from service.

During the early 2000s, Honda's Pan European ST1100 and ST1300 models were popular for policing purposes. However, following the tragic death of a police motorcyclist in 2005 when his ST1300 crashed after becoming unstable at high speed, alternative models were sought. The subsequent inquest heard that the Pan European's centre of gravity had been affected by the additional police equipment which had been fitted, which caused a condition identified as 'high-speed weave'.

Today, UK forces mostly use the BMW R1200RT or Yamaha FJR1300 models as performance motorcycles, as well as a variety of off-road trials bikes for accessing hard to reach rural and off-road areas. Scooters are used for urban transport and parking enforcement duties: London's Metropolitan Police built up a sizeable fleet of Piaggio MP3 three-wheeled scooters for patrolling red routes in the Capital as well as general traffic duties.

Of interest is the Metropolitan Police's Special Escort Group (SEG) which currently uses BMW R1200RS motorcycles for the armed escort of convoys and vehicles including the Royal Family, senior government members, visiting heads of state and similar dignitaries. Several features make this motorcycle fleet of interest, which include:

- A plain white livery with small Metropolitan Police logos on the panniers
- Fitted with blue lights but no sirens – riders use high-pitched whistles to make their presence known
- Police motorcyclists are Authorised Firearms Officers, overtly carrying their weapons
- The use of the letters 'SEG' within the registration of each motorcycle

A Gwent Police Honda Pan European ST1300, seen on a wet June day in 2007.

British Transport Police 2010 Yamaha FJR1300 (LX10 CRJ) on duty at the Epsom Derby on 1 June 2013. This model produced 144 bhp and had a top speed of 154 mph.

The BMW R1200RT is a popular choice for UK police forces. Two of the Metropolitan Police's fleet are seen at Horse Guards Parade for Trooping the Colour on 13 June 2015.

Produced by BMW Motorrad, the motorcycle division of BMW, the 2024 model BMW R1250RT-P is specifically designed for policing purposes and includes various options for blue lights, siren systems and other emergency equipment to meet each police force's individual requirements.

Air Support Units

The National Police Air Service (NPAS) became operational on 1 October 2012, taking over existing air support units from those police forces which had been operating their own helicopters. NPAS is currently headquartered at West Yorkshire Police's HQ in Wakefield. With a mission to tackle criminality, save lives and keep people and communities safe, an average flying speed of 130–150 knots means airborne officers can be above a scene quickly, saving vital minutes when searching for vulnerable persons or tracking high-speed vehicle pursuits. In 2023, NPAS reported an average response time of twelve minutes and eighteen seconds to reach an incident.

NPAS operates a fleet of twenty-four aircraft from its fifteen bases across England and Wales (sixteen Eurocopter EC135 helicopters, four EC145 helicopters and four Vulcanair P68 fixed-wing aircraft) and supports all territorial police forces and the British Transport Police across England and Wales. Separate from NPAS, Police Scotland's Air Support Unit operates a single Airbus H145 helicopter from New Glasgow Heliport, whilst the Police Service of Northern Ireland Air Support Unit operates independently from Aldergrove near Antrim with three helicopters (one Eurocopter EC135 and two EC145) and two fixed-wing aircraft (a Britten-Norman Islander and a Britten-Norman Defender).

The most common NPAS aircraft is the twin-engined Eurocopter EC135. Since being taken over by Airbus in 2014, newer examples are now known as the Airbus H135. The twin-engined police version of the EC135/H135 weighs in at 2,900 kg, with sufficient space for transporting armed officers or a police dog and handler to a scene. It has a maximum passenger capacity of seven and fuel sufficient for just under 400 miles, which offers between two and three hours of flying time. Police helicopters are fitted with day and night vision cameras, including high-definition thermal imaging infrared cameras with multiple zoom capabilities. Impressively, these allow for vehicle registrations to be read from two miles away. They also have computer systems to capture, record and encrypt camera footage, and securely transmit this data down to police officers on the ground.

Several EC145 helicopters have been introduced to NPAS and are primarily allocated to the London area in support of the Metropolitan Police, flying from Lippitts Hill and North Weald. The main differences with the EC145 are its larger size, a maximum passenger capacity of nine and a pair of more powerful Turbomeca Arriel engines providing up to 420 miles of range. After the Airbus merger, the EC145 became the H145 and at the time of writing there is only one H145 in police service, with the Police Scotland Air Support Unit.

A police helicopter is flown by a single civilian pilot, who has no policing powers, the majority being former military pilots with extensive low-level helicopter flying experience.

NPAS Benson Eurocopter EC135 P2+ G-TVHB was delivered to Thames Valley Police in October 2010 and joined the NPAS fleet on 1 October 2012. This August 2014 view shows it landing at Thames Valley Police's Sulhamstead HQ.

G-CPAS is a 2010 Eurocopter EC135 P2+, which before the formation of NPAS was flown by Cleveland Police from January 2011. In July 2016 it was flying as NPAS15 from Redhill (seen here hovering over Maidstone in Kent) and currently operates from Exeter in Devon as NPAS44.

They are joined by two Tactical Flight Officers (TFO) who are sworn police officers: the front seat observer has responsibility for task management and surveillance systems, whilst the rear seat observer is responsible for navigation, communications and downlinking.

The four NPAS Vulcanair P68 aircraft are based at East Midlands Airport and provide support to all police forces in England and Wales, except the Metropolitan Police. Each aircraft can remain airborne for up to eight hours, sufficient to cover an entire shift, and has a cruising speed of 120–140 knots. Due to weight restrictions, each aircraft carries one TFO.

New to Thames Valley Police in 2002 as G-CPSH, this NPAS Eurocopter EC135 T2+ was re-registered to G-POLC in 2016. It is seen returning to its base at Barton Aerodrome near Manchester in September 2023.

Drones

A drone is any vehicle that is operated remotely, rather than by an onboard pilot, and for policing purposes an increasing number of forces now have an aerial drone capability. Being quicker to deploy and more cost- effective than requesting assistance from the nearest NPAS helicopter, police drones can be fitted with a variety of equipment including high-powered cameras, thermal imaging, lights and speakers.

Drones can legally be flown to a maximum height of 120 metres (400 feet), which is the limit set by the Civil Aviation Authority to avoid interference with aircraft. With a ground speed of between 20 and 40 mph, a single battery charge allows between 30 and 45 minutes of flying time, dependent upon the specific model. This capability allows police drones to cover large areas on a single battery and provide live feeds to officers on the ground, ideal for search and rescue, covert surveillance and crowd control activities, amongst other tasks.

North Wales Police operates several drones; this one was seen operating near Colwyn Bay.

Marine Policing Units

Whilst many police forces either own or will have access to vessels such as Rigid Inflatable Boats (RIBs), far fewer of them have dedicated Marine Policing Units (MPUs). The largest marine unit within the UK is operated by the Ministry of Defence Police, a force that is featured later in this book.

Next in size is the Metropolitan Police's Marine Policing Unit which is based on the River Thames at Wapping, a site first used for river policing in 1798. Renamed the Thames River Police in 1800, it merged with the Metropolitan Police in 1839. This specialist unit of qualified police coxswains patrols nearly 50 miles of the Thames (and responds to incidents on other waterways in Greater London) twenty-four hours a day. They work in partnership with the Royal National Lifeboat Institution and the London Fire Brigade, both of whom also operate emergency boats on the River Thames. In 2020, six replacement vessels were ordered from Oy Botnia Marin Ab in Finland for five 'Targa 32' fast patrol boats and one larger 'Targa 37' command and control craft. The new Targa craft joined a service fleet of more than twenty boats, which includes fast RIBs in three different sizes, and Zodiac Milpro inflatable boats which can be deployed to smaller inland waterways. Other UK marine policing units include:

Essex Police's Marine Unit: Formed in 1949, and which patrols 562 miles of coast and waterways from Crayford Ness on the River Thames to the River Stour at Manningtree, including the port areas of Harwich, Tilbury and London Gateway, using launch boat 'Alert IV' and RIB 'Sentinel'.

Dorset Police's Marine Section: Patrolling 88 miles of Dorset coastline as well as the county's inland waterways. In 2020, the service took delivery of a 10.5-metre all-weather RIB 'Buccaneer', built by Ribcraft, and stationed at Poole Quay. Buccaneer has a top speed of 50 knots, and its 600-litre fuel tank provides an operating range of 200 miles.

Police Scotland's Marine Policing Unit: Located at four strategic locations around Scotland: two (Aberdeen and Greenock) are staffed by dedicated Marine and Diving Officers, with the other two being operated by non-dedicated Marine Officers. The unit deploys Delta Marine RHIB craft.

The Hampshire and Isle of Wight Police Marine Support Unit: Policing the Solent and its 253 miles of coastline, one of the busiest stretches of water in Europe. In 2012, Hampshire announced a £1.5 million investment in four new vessels including 'Commander' (a 12-metre catamaran for command, control and search purposes), 'Preventer' (a general-purpose launch boat) and 'Pursuer' and 'Protector' (a pair of 8-metre high-speed tactical RIBs). In 2019, the two larger boats were withdrawn as they were assessed to no longer be meeting operational needs.

Left: Prior to receiving the all-weather RIB 'Buccaneer' in 2020, Dorset Police's Marine Policing Unit used patrol boat *Alarm*, seen returning to Poole Quay in February 2006.

Below: Metropolitan Police Targa 31 *John Herriott IV* (MP2) patrols the River Thames near Tower Bridge in August 2016. John Herriott (1745–1817) was an English seafarer who founded the first Marine Police Force in London in 1798.

In June 2006, Hampshire Constabulary operated a trio of Mitchell 31 launches in the Solent. Seen here is *Lord Ashburton*, the other two were named *Sir James Scott* and *Earl Mountbatten of Burma*.

Also policing the Solent in June 2006 was Hampshire Constabulary Avon Rigid Inflatable Boat (RIB) *James Ward*.

Special Police Forces

Within the United Kingdom, 'Special Police Forces' are defined within specific legislation: (a) the Serious Organised Crime and Police Act 2005, (b) the Police, Public Order and Criminal Justice (Scotland) Act 2006 or (c) the Police and Justice Act 2006. Each of them is the responsibility of a specific government department (separate from the Home Office who oversee the territorial police forces within the UK) and each has responsibilities and duties related to a specific scope or activity across the whole of the country. There are three such Special Police Forces: the British Transport Police, the Civil Nuclear Constabulary and the Ministry of Defence Police.

British Transport Police

The British Transport Police (BTP) is responsible for policing the rail networks of England, Scotland and Wales, including more than 10,000 miles of track and over 3,000 premises (stations, depots, etc.). In addition to its responsibility to Network Rail, the BTP also polices:

- London Underground
- Docklands Light Railway
- London Trams (previously known as Croydon Tramlink)
- London's IFS Cloud Cable Car (previously known as the Emirates Air Line)
- West Midlands Metro
- Glasgow Subway
- Part of the Tyne and Wear Metro (the Sunderland branch, which uses Network Rail infrastructure)
- Eurostar international services, in conjunction with the French Police aux Frontières

For completeness, the BTP does not protect:

- The remainder of the Tyne and Wear Metro (policed by Northumbria Police)
- Manchester Metrolink (policed by Greater Manchester Police)
- Any heritage or historic railways (policed by the local territorial force)

The BTP's history started in June 1826, when a small contingent of police was introduced to the Stockton & Darlington Railway, and by 1838 employee 'policemen' were noted on the London, Birmingham & Liverpool Railway. The 1947 Transport Act created the British

Transport Commission, with the mission of creating a nationalised, integrated public transport system after the Second World War. Its responsibilities included buses, docks, railways, road haulage, shipping, tramways and inland waterways, amongst other activities. It was the British Transport Commission Act of 1949 that resulted in the merging of the existing pre-nationalised railway police forces, creating the British Transport Commission Police.

The British Transport Commission survived until early 1963, and when abolished the railway police operations were renamed British Transport Police. Until 1990, the BTP continued to police several docks and ports, including providing immigration services at smaller ports. The response to the London terrorist bombings of 7 July 2005 saw significant BTP involvement, and in 2011 the force introduced its own armed capabilities.

For conventional police patrol vehicles, the BTP has used similar vehicles to territorial police forces, which in the period covered by this publication includes the Ford Focus, Ford Kuga, Ford Mondeo, Ford Transit, Land Rover Defender, Land Rover Discovery, Leyland DAF/LDV, Nissan Pathfinder, Nissan Terrano, Peugeot 406, Peugeot Expert, Renault Espace, Renault Scenic, Renault Trafic, Skoda Octavia, Vauxhall Astra, Vauxhall Combo, Vauxhall Vivaro and Volvo V70, amongst many others. Examples of some of the BTP's more unusual police vehicles are included in the photographs in this section.

The British Transport Police built up a sizeable fleet of Peugeot vehicles, including the Peugeot 406 HDI. X46 LGU is seen at Birmingham New Street Station in May 2003.

In 2004, the BTP took delivery of three Renault Grand Espace 3.5 V6 cars, which were fitted out as Specialist Response Units to detect and respond to different types of terrorist threats and incidents in Central London. Note the dual lightbars fitted to the roof.

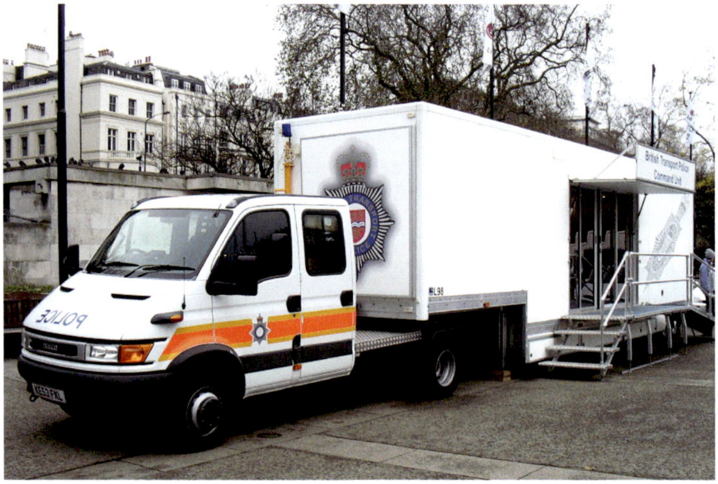

Also in 2004, the British Transport Police took delivery of a pair of Iveco Daily crew cab mini-articulated units. One of the pair, KE53 FKL, is seen towing the Force's Command Unit trailer in support of an operation at London's Marble Arch on 23 December 2004.

The other Iveco Daily crew cab used by the British Transport Police was KE53 FKM, which was towing the Force's mobile Custody Unit in December 2004. The BTP only has limited custody suites of its own, so benefitted from having a mobile unit to support incidents at different London locations.

In 2005, the British Transport Police added a pair of Iveco Daily Rescue Tenders to its Central London fleet. KE05 JLV, seen in May 2015 in Surrey Street, carried a 'B' fleet number denoting the London and the South East Division.

As noted elsewhere in this book, the British Transport Police has one of the largest police dog sections in the country. 2009 Ford Transit EO59 HRE was nearly new when seen in this March 2010 view visiting the Force Training Centre at Tadworth in Surrey.

The BTP operates a fleet of Emergency Intervention Units, driven by a police officer and providing emergency attendance at incidents for Network Rail Mobile Operations Managers or Engineers to reduce delays on the rail network. Essential railway repair equipment is carried in the rear. Ford Ranger LD68 KWY was observed near London Bridge in August 2022.

The combination of a British Transport Police Medic and a London Underground Network Incident Response Manager creates a 'Network Incident Response Team'. Mercedes-Benz Vito OU70 EDX is seen attending a fatality incident at Stratford station in East London in May 2024.

BTP: Emergency Response Units

London Underground has a fleet of Emergency Response Units (ERU) based at Camden, Acton, Battersea and Stratford which are operated by Transport for London. Available 24 hours a day, they are deployed to support the emergency services at the scene of incidents, and their personnel are engineers qualified to work on live tracks, having extensive mechanical and engineering knowledge and skills.

An initial batch of JDC-bodied Mercedes-Benz Ategos entered service in 2007, these being replaced by newer Volvo FLs in 2017 and 2018. Looking similar to fire appliances, these vehicles carry a large equipment set, including hydraulic jacks, chain and disc saws, airbags, stretchers, torches and a comprehensive toolkit. Whilst most of the later ERUs carry a TfL Emergency colour scheme and have amber lights, vehicles at two of the locations have reversible liveries which allow for them to become British Transport Police-liveried vehicles, able to respond to emergencies on blue lights and sirens when driven by a trained BTP response driver.

British Transport Police liveried Emergency Response Unit WX07 NWB is from the first batch of ERUs, carrying JDC bodywork on a 2007 Mercedes-Benz Atego chassis. This example carried permanent BTP livery and responded on blue lights and sirens to emergency incidents whilst being driven by a BTP response driver. It was noted at Waterloo Underground station in April 2012.

With its BTP fleet number and part of its police Battenburg livery visible in this view, KS66 XZX is seen operating as a Transport for London/London Underground Emergency Response Unit (2611) at Stratford bus station on 30 May 2024. It is a 2017 Volvo FL with JDC rescue tender bodywork and has interchangeable livery panels.

Civil Nuclear Constabulary

The Civil Nuclear Constabulary (CNC) was created in 2005 under the Energy Act of 2004 and replaced the previous UK Atomic Energy Authority Constabulary (UKAEAC) which had been in existence since 1955. The CNC has a remit to provide policing and security at relevant civil nuclear sites, and for the security of nuclear materials in transit between sites. The CNC does not provide protection for the UK's nuclear weapons, which remain the responsibility of the Armed Forces and the Ministry of Defence Police. The current jurisdiction of the CNC includes facilities at Culham (also the CNC headquarters), Dounreay, Dungeness, Hartlepool, Harwell, Heysham, Hinkley Point, Hunterston, Sellafield, Sizewell and Torness. All operational CNC officers are Authorised Firearms Officers and are routinely armed whilst on duty.

Marked vehicles used by the CNC (and the former UKAEAC) within the period covered in this book included the Ford Focus, Ford Granada, Ford Ranger, Ford S-MAX and Ford Transit, Land Rover Defenders and Discoveries. More recently, the BMW X5, Skoda Kodiaq and Ovik Crossway have joined their fleet list: the last of these being ballistically protected. CNC, which

Seen in June 2002 with the UK Atomic Energy Authority Constabulary is 2000 Land Rover Discovery X985 SRM. Note the spotlight mounted on top of the lightbar.

In May 2005 the UKAEAC had recently become the Civil Nuclear Constabulary. 2001 Ford Focus PX51 DDE carries the new logos and website address.

The Civil Nuclear Constabulary used the Mitsubishi Shogun Sport as convoy escort vehicles. PX05 AEP is a 2005 example with half-Battenburg markings.

operates over a hundred vehicles, has joined the Chiltern Transport Consortium (CTC), which provides centralised vehicle procurement and maintenance services for Bedfordshire Police, Hertfordshire Constabulary and Thames Valley Police.

Ministry of Defence Police

Part of the UK's Ministry of Defence, the Ministry of Defence Police (MDP) has responsibility for protecting Ministry of Defence sites, personnel and infrastructure across the United Kingdom – including GCHQ in Gloucestershire and the Atomic Weapons Establishment in Berkshire. Headquartered at RAF Wyton in Cambridgeshire, the MDP is a civilian Special Police Force (and not military police) and has over 2,500 officers, many of whom are Authorised Firearms Officers.

The origins of the MDP can be traced back to 1923, when the Special Constables Act resulted in the creation of the Air Force Department Constabulary, the Admiralty Constabulary and the Army Department Constabulary. These three separate organisations merged in 1971, with the creation of the MDP.

The MDP has an interesting and varied fleet of police vehicles. In 1996, for example, they took delivery of a batch of four armoured Glover Webb Tactica patrol vehicles for the Atomic Weapons Establishment in Berkshire, each capable of transporting eight armed personnel. Fitted with two-wheel drive (instead of standard four-wheel drive) for higher road speeds, the Tacticas were powered by 6-litre turbocharged Perkins engines coupled to a five-speed Allison automatic geabox. All four have since been withdrawn.

The Special Escort Group of the MDP is responsible for the security of defence nuclear materials being transported by road. Several times a year, some of the UK's Trident nuclear weapons are transported 450 miles by road between the Atomic Weapons Establishment in Berkshire and the Royal Naval Armaments Depot at Coulport in Argyll, Scotland, where they are loaded onto (or removed from) Vanguard class Royal Navy submarines. These movements involve dozens of specialist vehicles from the MDP and a significant complement of vehicles and heavily armed personnel from the UK's Armed Forces to protect these sizeable convoys, which can occasionally be disrupted by traffic, bad weather, accidents or protesters.

In 2021, a £36 million order for eighteen patrol craft was placed with Marine Specialised Technology of Birkenhead, sixteen for the MDP and two for the Gibraltar Defence Police. Delivered in 2022, each of these 15-metre patrols vessels has a crew of three, is powered by water jet engines to a top speed of 30 knots and is fitted with CCTV systems and bulletproof protection. They are deployed to protect assets and detect threats at naval bases including Portsmouth, Devonport and Clyde, as well as the Gibraltar Naval Dockyard which is protected by the Gibraltar Defence Police.

With many locations to protect across the UK, it is no surprise that the MDP requires a large and diverse fleet of vehicles, drawn from almost all manufacturers who supply the UK police vehicle market; the selection of photographs in this section includes some of the more unusual. MDP vehicles will mostly carry Battenburg liveries or plain green military-style colours; their Battenburg vehicles look similar to those from territorial police forces to a bystander.

Glover Webb Tactica 159 (N855 GBK) was one of four delivered to the Ministry of Defence Police in 1996. Its heavily armoured bodywork carried up to eight fully armed officers.

The Ministry of Defence Police has been a significant user of the Land Rover Defender and Discovery. Seen at Bordon, Hampshire, is R61 YVW, a 1997 Land Rover Defender TDI.

Ministry of Defence Police 141 (T759 LJN) is a 1999 Leyland DAF 55, which has been fitted out as one of the Force's mobile Command Units.

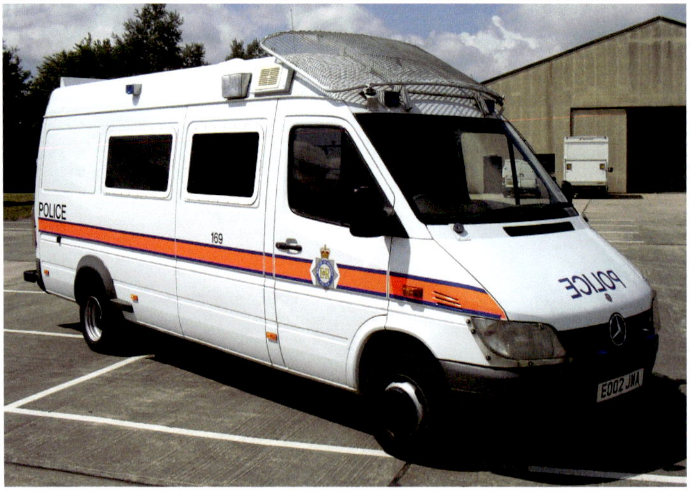

Ministry of Defence Police 169 (E002 JWA), a heavily protected 2002 Mercedes-Benz Sprinter.

Ministry of Defence Police 267 (EU03 FHH), a 2003 Mitsubishi Space Star 1.9D. This is a vehicle type that was rarely seen as a marked police vehicle in the UK.

Ministry of Defence Police 408, a 2007 Volkswagen Sharan, in half-Battenburg livery.

Ministry of Defence Police EY20 UXT, a 2020 Citroen Relay seen in Whitehall, London.

Ministry of Defence Police 787 (RK20 EEV), a 2020 Land Rover Discovery Sport ARV.

Parks Police

Many parks and open spaces within the London area have small constabularies with responsibility for specific policing matters, including the enforcement of local byelaws within their specific jurisdictions. In all cases, the statutory responsibility for policing, including more serious incidents, remains with the local territorial police force, which is almost exclusively the Metropolitan Police (or Essex Police for part of Epping Forest).

Several parks police services were abolished during the period covered by this book. The most notable of these was the Royal Parks Constabulary (RPC), established in 1872 as the Royal Parks Keepers to protect the Royal Parks in London and Edinburgh. London's Hyde Park was added to their responsibilities in 1993, having previously been policed by the Metropolitan Police. On 1 April 2004, following a review, the RPC's London duties were absorbed into the Metropolitan Police's Royal Parks Operational Command Unit, and its Scottish duties were taken over by Historic Scotland, supported by Lothian and Borders Police.

Other London parks police services disbanded in recent years include Barking and Dagenham Parks Police (2010), Brent Parks Constabulary (late 1990s), Greenwich Parks Constabulary (2001), Hammersmith and Fulham Parks Constabulary (2021), Haringey Parks Constabulary (2009), Hillingdon Parks Patrol Service (2016), Newham Community Constabulary (2009), Redbridge Parks Police (2011) and Sutton Parks Constabulary (2007).

There are six parks police services currently in operation:

Epping Forest Keepers enforce the Epping Forest Act of 1878 and associated byelaws within the 10 square miles of Epping Forest in east London. Managed by the City of London Corporation, the small number of Forest Keepers (who are attested constables) are employees. Three 2019 Mitsubishi Outlander PHEV (plug-in hybrid) vehicles are currently in use, each carrying half-Battenburg livery and 'Epping Forest Constables'.

Hampstead Heath Constabulary was formed in 1992 to patrol London's Hampstead Heath, which is administered by the City of London Corporation. Personnel are attested as constables under Article 18 of the Greater London Parks and Open Spaces Act of 1967. Recent marked police vehicles used include a 2011 Ford Transit Connect, a 2015 Vauxhall Mokka and a 2019 Mitsubishi Outlander.

Havering Parks Constabulary dates from 2016, when the London Borough of Havering voted to attest its existing Parks Protection Officers under Article 18 of the Greater London Parks and Open Spaces Act of 1967. Their jurisdiction is limited to Havering's parks and open spaces. Marked vehicles are used – a single 2011 Ford Ranger with full vehicle Battenburg livery and a pair of 2011 Kawasaki KLX250 off-road motorcycles.

Kew Constabulary (formed as the Royal Botanic Gardens Constabulary in 1845) polices the 330 acres of the Royal Botanic Gardens at Kew, near Richmond upon Thames. Officers have powers under Section 3 of the Parks Regulation Act of 1872. Marked police vehicles include a 2009 Honda Accord and a 2019 Kia Nero.

Royal Borough of Kensington and Chelsea Parks Police was formed in 1991, with officers attested under Article 18 of the Greater London Parks and Open Spaces Act of 1967 to police the borough's parks and open spaces. In 2013, it merged with Hammersmith and Fulham Parks Constabulary, forming the Parks Police Service, which lasted until 2019 when RBKCPP returned to being a single service. Marked police vehicles seeing service included a 2003 Nissan X-Trail Sport, a pair of 2014 Dacia Dusters and most recently a 2023 all-electric Toyota bZ4X, the first liveried use of this model in UK policing.

Wandsworth Parks and Events Police are responsible for policing the many parks and open spaces within the London Borough of Wandsworth. Created in 1984 as Wandsworth Parks Police, its constables were attested under the Greater London Parks and Open Spaces Order of 1967 and worked closely with the Metropolitan Police. In 2012, Wandsworth Council elected to establish a Metropolitan Police 'Safer Parks Team', effectively abolishing Wandsworth Parks Police, although the Council retained five officers to form the new Wandsworth Events Police Service. In 2015, following challenges with anticipated cost savings, the service was rebranded as Wandsworth Parks and Events Police. Recent marked vehicles used by Wandsworth include the Renault Megane, Renault Kangoo, Mercedes-Benz Vito, Ford Transit, Ford Transit Connect and Ford C-MAX.

Royal Parks Constabulary 1999 Land Rover Discovery TD5 V479 LAM was photographed in Richmond Park in June 2002. The service was taken over by the Metropolitan Police in April 2004.

Sutton's Parks Constabulary operated between 1998 and 2007. The marked fleet included an Isuzu Trooper, this 1998 Ford Transit, and a pair of Suzuki DRZ 400 trials bikes.

Royal Borough of Kensington and Chelsea Parks Police acquired this Nissan X-Trail Sport in 2003. KE53 JDX carries half-Battenburg livery and notes that it is video equipped.

Hampstead Heath Constabulary uses this 2015 Vauxhall Mokka within their fleet, a model rarely purchased by UK police forces. It was undertaking a routine patrol on Hampstead Heath in this March 2019 view.

Wandsworth Parks Police were using LPG-powered Renault Meganes as patrol vehicles in the early 2000s. V214 ELC is a 1999 model, carrying a distinctive green and blue stripe.

By 2010, Wandsworth Parks Police had acquired a pair of Ford C-MAX vehicles for patrolling its various parks. LC08 KTX is a 2008 example, carrying half-Battenburg livery.

Currently known as Wandsworth Parks and Events Police, the latest addition to the fleet at the time of writing is 2016 Ford Transit LF16 NPO, pictured in September 2020.

Ports Police

Most commercial ports in the United Kingdom have police officers sworn in under the Harbours, Docks and Piers Clauses Act of 1847. Section 79 of the Act allows them to be sworn in as Special Constables, giving them the full powers of a constable on any land owned by the port, harbour or dock and up to a mile from it. The Marine Navigation Act of 2013 enables ports to use their constables to act beyond that 1-mile limit (in relation to port policing matters) where the local Chief Constable has provided specific consent. Serious incidents would normally become the responsibility of the local territorial police force.

There are nine such police forces within the UK today:

Belfast Harbour Police was formed in 1847 under the Belfast Harbour Act, covering the 2,000-acre Belfast Harbour estate and up to a mile from it. Belfast Harbour Police vehicles have included Ford Galaxy, Kia Sportage, Skoda Kodiaq and Volkswagen Tiguan cars, Land Rover Discovery and Freelander 4×4s, as well as police launch *Bowstead,* named after John Bowstead, the first Police Constable appointed to protect Belfast city's quays in 1824.

Port of Bristol Police was established under the Bristol Docks Act of 1803, with a jurisdiction that includes the Avonmouth Docks, Royal Portbury Docks and trading estates which are owned by the Bristol Port Company. Marked police vehicles have included the Ford Escort, Mitsubishi Shogun, Range Rover, Land Rover Discovery and Freelander, and more recently the Ford Kuga.

Port of Dover Police was formed in 1933, and is maintained under the Dover Harbour Consolidation Act of 1954, being funded by the Dover Harbour Board. The Board owns significant land along Dover seafront, including ferry and cruise terminals, as well as the nearby Port Zone: this gives the Port of Dover Police authority across much of the town, although most of their work is focused on the Eastern and Western Terminals. Since 2000, the marked vehicle fleet has included Fords (Focus, Mondeo and Ranger), Renault Master and Trafic vans, a Land Rover Discovery and a Peugeot Expert: the current fleet comprises a Toyota RAV4, Mercedes-Benz Vito and Ford Transit vans. A RIB is used to patrol within the dock area and along the neighbouring shorelines.

Falmouth Docks Police came about as a result of the Falmouth Docks Act of 1959, although an earlier Falmouth Harbour Police had been created in 1870, with a jurisdiction covering

Falmouth Docks in Cornwall and a mile around them. This is a small police force funded by A&P Falmouth, the dockyard operator, and their activities are more closely aligned to those of a security company. No marked police response vehicles are known to be in use at the time of writing.

Port of Felixstowe Police came into being in 1975, as permitted by the Felixstowe Dock and Railway Act 1956. Felixstowe Dock and Railway Police, as they were originally known, are sworn Special Constables with police powers at the Port of Felixstowe, which is the UK's largest port, and up to a mile from it. The Port Police are supported by private security personnel. The small fleet of police vehicles used at Felixstowe has included Ford Escorts, Focuses and Transits.

Port of Liverpool Police was created by the Mersey Docks and Harbour (Police) Order of 1975 and came into being in June of that year. Policing powers extend throughout the estates of the Liverpool, Bootle and Birkenhead Docks, and up to a mile beyond those perimeters. Of note is the force's crest which includes the word 'Manchester' reflecting that the Port of Liverpool Police also patrol the Manchester Ship Canal, which until 1993 was the responsibility of the Manchester Ship Canal Police. Recent marked police vehicles have included the Toyota Hilux and Nissan Navara, and previously a Land Rover Defender was used between 2010 and 2013.

Port of Portland Police on the Isle of Portland in Dorset is one of the country's newest police forces, being established by the Portland Harbour Revision Order of 1997. Portland Harbour is operated by Langham Industries, who took control from the Royal Navy in 1997, and the site now manages cruise ships, cargo and bunker vessels, as well as ships from the Royal Navy and Royal Fleet Auxiliary. Police officers are responsible for enforcing the Portland Port General Byelaws of 2018. Marked police vehicles include the Land Rover Discovery.

Tees and Hartlepool Port Authority Harbour Police was formed on 18 January 1904, and the ongoing authority of the police force is derived from the Tees and Hartlepool Port Authority Act 1966. Funded by PD Ports, police officers have powers within Teesport, which is located on the River Tees. A variety of marked vehicles have been operated within the period covered by this book, including Ford Focus, Ford Mondeo, Ford Ranger, Ford Transit, Peugeot 308 and 406, Skoda Octavia and Vauxhall Vivaro: the current fleet uses the Skoda Kodiaq.

The Port of Tilbury Police is responsible for policing both the Port of Tilbury and 'Tilbury 2' in Essex, owned by the Port of Tilbury Limited, a subsidiary of Forth Ports plc. Originally formed in 1909 as the Port of London Authority Police (under the Port of London Authority Act of 1908), for many years PLA Police protected all of London's commercial docks. In 1992, the PLA Police was restructured, downsized and limited to just the Port of Tilbury: at that point the policing of all other London Docks became the responsibility of the Metropolitan Police's Marine Support Unit. Marked vehicles have included the Ford Mondeo, Ford S-MAX, Ford Transit and a single Lexus RX350, with more recent additions including the Hyundai i30 and Hyundai Santa Fe.

1998 Ford Transit R288 HJN was one of a pair of marked vehicles being operated by the Port of Tilbury Police in Essex when seen in this June 2004 photograph.

The Port of Dover Police in Kent operated several Ford Mondeo patrol vehicles at the turn of the century: GK51 NYT is a diesel-engined Ford Mondeo LX from 2001.

The Port of Felixstowe in Suffolk is the UK's largest port and is protected by the Port of Felixstowe Police. This September 2005 view is of their 2003 Ford Focus, AY03 OFK.

Other Police Forces

Belfast International Airport Constabulary

Belfast International Airport Constabulary (BIAC) is a specialist police force with responsibility for protecting Belfast International Airport at Aldergrove in Northern Ireland. Formed under the Airports (Northern Ireland) Order 1994, this privately funded force has officers who are employees of the airport authority. More serious incidents within the airport's perimeter are passed on to the Police Service of Northern Ireland. BIAC-marked police vehicles operated at Aldergrove include Mitsubishi Shogun 4×4s and Volkswagen Crafter vans.

Cambridge University Constabulary

Cambridge University Constabulary appoints constables under the Universities Act of 1825: the Chancellor and Vice-Chancellor of the University of Cambridge have the authority to appoint constables for a one-year period on 1 October each year, and contracts can be renewed. Constables have policing powers within a 5-mile radius of Great St Mary's Church. Whilst included here for completeness, at the time of writing it is not thought that this constabulary operates any marked police vehicles.

Mersey Tunnels Police

Privately funded by Merseytravel, the Mersey Tunnels Police is a specialist force formed in 1936 that polices the Mersey Tunnels together with their approach and exit roads. Accountable to the Merseyside Passenger Transport Executive, it has more than fifty officers with powers from Section 105 of the County of Merseyside Act of 1980 who are responsible for enforcing Mersey Tunnels byelaws. Mersey Tunnels Police only recruits officers who have current or previous policing experience.

For a small police force, the Mersey Tunnels Police has an interesting and varied fleet which normally exceeds ten vehicles at any one time. At the start of this century, these included the Ford Galaxy and Land Rover Discovery, with the more recent fleet including BMW X3, Volvo V60, XC60 and XC70, Land Rover Discovery and a Mercedes-Benz Vito used as a cell van.

The Mersey Tunnels Police is privately funded by Merseytravel and has jurisdiction over the two Mersey road tunnels, including their approach and exit roads. This February 2010 view shows 2002 Land Rover Discovery TD5 (DE52 CVV) on the approach to the Queensway Tunnel.

DK06 WBP is a 2006 Ford Galaxy used by the Mersey Tunnels Police in Liverpool. It is seen in February 2010 at the Queensway Tunnel attending to a call from a member of the public at the adjacent Mersey Tunnel Police Information Point.

Above left: Mersey Tunnels Police operate a cell van for conveying arrested persons to the local custody suites of Merseyside Police. DK14 ANP, a 2014 Mercedes-Benz Vito, was photographed in March 2017.

Above right: PE15 WWS is one of a pair of 2015 Land Rover Discovery Incident Response Vehicles delivered to Mersey Tunnels Police in 2015, seen here in March 2017.

UK Service (Military) Police

Each branch of the UK military operates its own service police, with service police personnel having jurisdiction over serving military personnel and any civilians included within the Armed Forces Act of 2006. They have no police powers over the wider public. Whilst service police can investigate all crimes within their jurisdiction, within the UK the most serious of crimes will be passed to the local territorial police force.

Royal Military Police

The Royal Military Police (RMP) provides policing and investigation services for the British Army within the UK and wherever its personnel are deployed overseas for operational reasons or on exercise. The RMP can trace its recent origins to 1877 as the Military Mounted Police, followed in 1885 by the Military Foot Police: the two merged in 1926 to form the Corps of Military Police. The RMP is headed by a Colonel Commandant and is headquartered at MOD Southwick Park near Portsmouth. Aside from policing within the service community (which includes reciprocal jurisdiction over both Royal Navy and Royal Air Force personnel), the RMP provides assistance to territorial police forces within garrison towns, including Aldershot, Catterick, Colchester, Warminster, etc.

Prior to adopting the blue and yellow Battenburg scheme, the Royal Military Police used a blue-bordered single yellow stripe, as seen on this 2002 Vauxhall Corsa in Bordon, Hampshire.

Royal Military Police HX57 YOY, a Vauxhall Vectra 1.9 CTDi, is seen in April 2009 in half-Battenburg colours. Note the RMP roof code and Military Police lightbar.

The RMP operates a large fleet of marked police vehicles, which have included the Vauxhall Astra, Corsa and Vectra, the Ford Escort, Fiesta, Mondeo and Transit, Citroen C3, Kia Cee'd, Land Rover Defender, MG ZS and Skoda Superb. Green and camouflaged Army service vehicles are also used, mostly military-registered Land Rover Defenders, with the addition of a blue light and 'Military Police' plates to the front and rear. A wider variety of locally sourced vehicles may be seen overseas within countries where the RMP has been deployed.

Royal Navy Police

The Royal Navy Police (RNP) provides a policing and criminal investigation capability for the Royal Navy and Royal Marines within the UK, at sea and in several overseas areas. The RNP is headed by the Provost Marshal (Naval), based at HMS Excellent in Portsmouth. Previously known as the Royal Navy Regulating Branch until 2007 (hence personnel were known as 'Regulators'), it was renamed to the Royal Navy Police and the current service incorporated the Royal Marines Police in 2009. Whilst RNP personnel are not warranted constables, they have jurisdiction over Royal Navy personnel, as well as over Army and Royal Air Force personnel under reciprocal agreements. They have limited powers over civilians under certain circumstances within the territorial waters of England and Wales.

The annual Army vs Navy rugby match at Twickenham Stadium was the location for this photo of Royal Navy Police 2002 Ford Transit SN52 FXU on 28 April 2012.

Royal Navy Police Vauxhall Vivaro HV14 FCL was seen in Portsmouth in October 2015.

The RNP uses a variety of marked police vehicles, which have included the Vauxhall Astra, Ford Mondeo, Land Rover Discovery, Ford Transit, Peugeot Boxer and Vauxhall Vivaro, amongst others.

Royal Air Force Police

The Royal Air Force Police (RAFP) protects RAF bases, aircraft and personnel and is headed by the Provost Marshal of the Royal Air Force with the rank of Group Captain, based at RAF Honington. The RAFP was formed in 1918 from the merger of the Royal Flying Corps and the Royal Naval Air Service. As with the RMP and RNP, the RAFP has policing authority over personnel of the other armed services. Alongside policing and security tasks, the RAFP undertakes investigative work, VIP and aircraft protection, counter intelligence and cyber security operations. They are the only branch of Service Police to deploy police dogs.

The RAFP have a large fleet of marked police vehicles, which during the period covered by this book have changed their colour schemes from a single fluorescent orange stripe with a thin blue border to a single yellow stripe (with blue borders) and then onto half-Battenburg colours. Common marked vehicles in the fleet have included Fords (Focus, Ranger, Transit, etc.), Skoda Octavia, Toyota Hilux and Vauxhalls (Frontera, Corsa, Astra, etc.). Larger Citroen Relay dog vans are used for the movement of police dogs. Green and camouflaged RAF Land Rover Defenders are also used in quantity: these military-registered vehicles are fitted with single blue lights or a lightbar, and black and red 'RAF Police' signs to the front and rear.

Royal Air Force Police 2003 Vauxhall Astra Estate KE53 PZU, with 'RAF' roof markings.

Royal Air Force Land Rover Defender 45KF 44 was part of the RAF Police fleet – note the black and red police signage and full-width lightbar.

Crown Dependencies and British Overseas Territories

Whilst not part of the mainland United Kingdom, there are five additional police forces that are of interest and so are included here. Two of these, the States of Jersey Police and the States of Guernsey Police Service, are in the Channel Islands, as Crown Dependencies, as are Jersey's twelve smaller parish-based Honorary Police units. Also within a Crown Dependency is the Isle of Man Constabulary, and a little further afield the Royal Gibraltar Police and Gibraltar Defence Police operate within the British Overseas Territory of Gibraltar.

States of Jersey Police

Originating in 1854, the St Helier Paid Police Force was enlarged and started to provide twenty-four-hour service from the 1890s. The States of Jersey Police was named in 1960 and has operated in its current form since the Police Force (Jersey) Law of 1974. It is the only paid, island-wide police operation within the Bailiwick of Jersey. At the turn of this century, the States of Jersey Police fleet included Honda Civics and Streams, Vauxhall Corsas and Vectras, Land Rover Discoveries and Mercedes-Benz Sprinter vans. More recent additions have included the BMW 216D, 320D and electric BMW i3, Ford Transit, Land Rover Discovery 4, Mitsubishi Shogun, Skoda Citigo and Octavia and Volkswagen Caddy and Transporter vans. A Volkswagen Transporter is used as the island's Collision Investigation Unit, a Volkswagen Crafter as an Incident Command Vehicle and a DAF LF for prisoner transport. Motorcycles have included the Honda Crossrunner VFR800X and the Honda Deauville.

States of Jersey Police Honda Accord J96644, seen in St Helier in December 2003.

States of Jersey Police Land Rover Discovery J95059, seen at the since-closed Rouge Bouillion Police Station in St Helier. This vehicle later received the half-Battenburg style of police livery.

Jersey Honorary Police

Jersey's twelve parishes each have an unpaid Honorary Police (Police Honorifique), who deal with local policing matters within their respective parishes. There are typically only one or two marked vehicles used by the Honorary Police of each parish. By parish, these have included: St John (Dacia Duster), St Brelade (Ford C-MAX, Peugeot 407, Skoda Yeti and VW Transporter), St Saviour (Toyota Avensis, Honda CR-V and BMX X5), St Ouen (BMW X3), Grouville (Honda CR-V and Honda Accord), St Clement (Ford Fiesta, Honda CR-V and Mitsubishi Shogun), St Martin (Honda CR-V and Toyota Hilux), St Mary (Honda CR-V and Mitsubishi Shogun), St Lawrence (Skoda Octavia, Ford Transit Connect and Volkswagen Caddy), St Helier (Ford S-MAX, Honda CR-V and Volkswagen Transporter), St Peter (BMW 320D and BMW X3) and Trinity (Honda CR-V). A single Fiat Ducato mobile office/command unit is shared amongst all twelve parishes, being stationed in St Helier.

States of Guernsey Police Service

Parish constables have been part of the Bailiwick of Guernsey for several centuries, becoming uniformed in 1853, with the current police service starting in 1920. Today's States of Guernsey Police Service also provides policing services to the neighbouring islands of Alderney, Herm and Sark. Since 2015, all the islands' emergency calls for police, fire, ambulance and coastguard assistance are handled by the civilian-staffed Joint Emergency Services Control Centre (JESCC) located in St Peter Port. Alongside routine policing, the Service operates a police dog section, undertakes criminal and commercial fraud investigations and unusually for a police force provides a bomb disposal capability.

The author visited Guernsey in December 2003 and more recently in July 2019. In 2003, the simple colour scheme of two narrow orange stripes prevailed, and the marked fleet included BMW 320, Ford Focus, Ford Transit, Honda Civic, Toyota Hiace, Vauxhall Astravan (for police dogs), Land Rover Defender (including one as a Police Control Unit) and Honda Pan European ST1100 motorcycles. Fast forward to 2019, and the Battenburg-liveried fleet

States of Guernsey Police Service Land Rover Defender 41198, seen in a rainy St Peter Port in December 2003. Note the roof lighting arrangement and 'Island Police' name on the doors.

One of Guernsey's two BMW X5 Armed Response Vehicles on patrol in St Peter Port in July 2019. As the vehicle weighs in at over 2 tonnes unladen, it is restricted to a top speed of 25 mph when not responding to emergencies, as shown by the notice on the passenger door.

comprised the Skoda Fabia, Skoda Octavia, Mitsubishi L200, a pair of electric BMW i3s, BMW 330D, BMW X3, BMW X5 (as ARVs), Ford Transit and Honda FJR1300 motorcycles. Bomb disposal vehicles included a Toyota Hiace and more recently an Isuzu D-Max.

The nearby islands of Herm and Sark are both car free, so there are no police vehicles to record. Just two police vehicles are allocated to Alderney – a Nissan NV200 van and a Dacia Duster car, the latter carrying a local cherished registration of AY999.

Isle of Man Constabulary

The responsibility of the Minister of Home Affairs of the Isle of Man government, the Isle of Man Constabulary has its headquarters in Douglas and provides policing services to the island from four Neighbourhood Policing Teams. Specialist services are delivered by the Operational Support Group, providing armed officers, public order resources, search teams and trained negotiators.

The Isle of Man is known for its annual 'TT' (Tourist Trophy) motorcycle racing event, which has been staged each May and June since 1907. With a huge influx of motorcyclists each year, combined with the island having no national speed limit (other than where

Isle of Man Constabulary LMN-641-P is a 2014 Ford Focus ST, used on the island as a Collision Investigation Unit.

Isle of Man Constabulary Neighbourhood Policing Teams use Ford Transit and Mercedes-Benz Vito vans as patrol vehicles. Transit NMN-597-K was on duty in Douglas in September 2021.

Isle of Man Constabulary operates a small but varied fleet of motorcycles. PMN-613-B is a 2020 BMW R1250RT allocated to the island's Roads Policing Unit.

indicated), this provides the Roads Policing Unit (RPU) with interesting challenges, often requiring high-performance police cars and motorcycles to be deployed.

A recent visit to Douglas Police Station in September 2021 showed the fleet to include BMWs (325D and X5), Fords (Focus, Focus ST, Galaxy, Kuga, Mondeo and S-MAX), Hyundai i30, Land Rover Defender and Peugeot 308. Vans included the Ford Transit, Transit Connect and the Mercedes-Benz Vito, and the motorcycle fleet included the BMW R1250RT and Honda VFR 1200.

Royal Gibraltar Police

Gibraltar is a small British Overseas Territory, located at the southern tip of Spain where the Atlantic Ocean and the Mediterranean Sea meet. The 426-metre Rock of Gibraltar dominates its 2.6 square miles, and it is home to more than 30,000 Gibraltarians. The Gibraltar Police Force was formed in 1830, only months after the Metropolitan Police

Royal Gibraltar Police currently use a fleet of Kia Sportage cars for patrolling this small British Overseas Territory. G1098F was photographed in April 2023.

Royal Gibraltar Police's Command Support Unit is Mercedes-Benz Sprinter G9725D, which entered service in 2014. Seen in 2023, it is an inter-agency vehicle that is available for use by the Gibraltar Fire and Rescue Service and Gibraltar Ambulance Service when required.

in London. Queen Elizabeth II granted the royal prefix and the force become the Royal Gibraltar Police (RGP) in 1992. Until 1999, when St John Ambulance took over, RGP provided the only emergency ambulance service in Gibraltar. Its current headquarters is at New Mole House Police Station in Rosia Road.

The RGP uses the Royal Navy base for their police boats: the Marine Section has a fleet of four patrol boats, which as well as covering Gibraltar's shorelines are used to intercept drug traffickers and people smugglers attempting to cross the 8.5 miles from Morocco to Europe. The current marked vehicle fleet includes the Kia Sportage, Renault Trafic, Mitsubishi L200 (as ARVs) and a single Mercedes-Benz Sprinter as a Combined Support Unit, which is shared with Gibraltar's fire and rescue and ambulance services. The Honda CB500X makes up the current RGP motorcycle fleet.

Gibraltar Defence Police

The Gibraltar Defence Police (GDP) was formed in 2009, having previously been named the Gibraltar Services Police. It is a civilian police force providing policing and security services for Ministry of Defence operations in Gibraltar. The Chief of Police reports to the Commander of British Forces Gibraltar and is headquartered within the Naval Base. With similar operations to the UK's Ministry of Defence Police, all GDP officers are firearms trained and routinely armed, and a dog section was introduced in 2012. Recent marked vehicles used include the Lexus NX, Volkswagen Amarok and Renault Trafic and Master vans.

In June 2021, the *Gibraltar Chronicle* reported that the GDP would receive two new patrol boats, part of a £36 million order for eighteen patrol craft being built by Marine Specialised Technology of Birkenhead (the other sixteen being for the Ministry of Defence Police in the UK). Joining the GDP's two existing rigid-hull inflatable high-speed 'Arctic 24' interceptor boats, capable of 55 knots, the newest 15-metre vessels were delivered in mid-2022, each having a capacity for three crew, being powered to a maximum speed of 30 knots by water jet engines and fitted with CCTV systems and bulletproof protection.

Gibraltar Defence Police Renault Trafic 43RN63, seen crossing the runway of Gibraltar International Airport/Royal Air Force Gibraltar in April 2023. Note the Royal Navy military registration plates which are fitted to all Gibraltar Defence Police vehicles.

Looking to the Future

Having looked at the last twenty-five years of police vehicles, what changes can we expect over the next few years? Several police forces have compiled and published their police vehicle strategies for the period between now and 2030, and four common themes can be identified within many of them: (a) the increased availability of the right police vehicles in the right place at the right time, (b) the increased use of reliable vehicle-based technologies to support officers working from vehicles, (c) plans to reduce the environmental impact of police fleets and (d) exploring interoperability of police vehicles with other emergency services and authorities.

Increased Availability of Vehicles

Police forces need to have contingency vehicles available to support front-line policing activities. When vehicles are off the road with accident damage, for unscheduled repairs or planned maintenance, forces need to plan for a reserve stock of vehicles to keep their officers mobile. This supports the objective of having the right type of police vehicle available at the right place at the right time.

At the start of the century, individual police forces operated fleets which often comprised vehicles from many individual manufacturers. In turn, this required extensive maintenance knowledge of each type, and associated access to a larger stock of spare parts. Fleet standardisation, focusing on a smaller number of makes, has helped to improve maintenance activities and reduce costs. A need to drive proactive engagement with vehicle users (both police officers and civilian staff) will improve the timeliness and quality of vehicle fault reporting, to prevent more serious issues from developing.

Increased Use of Vehicle-Based Technologies

Today's police officer can complete much of their traditional 'paperwork' on touch-screen mobile electronic devices, meaning more vehicle-based remote working. With police vehicles increasingly used as mobile offices, they need secure systems and reliable data connectivity. A need to standardise additional vehicle assets including TETRA radio systems such as Airwave, ANPR and speed detection equipment, blue lights and sirens, video recording and electronic signage is reducing costs and expediting the replacement of faulty assets.

Understanding how and where a police vehicle is being driven, its fuel efficiency data and having advanced notice of vehicle faults are some of the benefits delivered by telematics systems. Telematics systems also record vehicle speed, acceleration and braking, and when emergency equipment has been activated. Improving police driver behaviour and vehicle fuel efficiency, combined with better information to investigate police vehicle incidents, means telematics are already playing an increasingly significant role.

The NAPFM has been working with the ACPO Vehicle Standardisation Group and Intelligent Transport System Group on initiatives in this area. For example, the 'One Box' single vehicle architecture (OBSVA) aims to integrate vehicle technologies with emergency service equipment and data management. It sets out the requirements for and testing of electrical systems to be fitted into emergency vehicles, both at original manufacture or as an aftermarket fit. The goal is to simplify the provision of power, the controlling of inputs and the processing of outputs from emergency equipment fitted to police vehicles, and where possible integrate these with original equipment installed by the vehicle manufacturer.

Reduction in the Environmental Impact of Vehicles

The UK has committed to becoming carbon net zero by 2050, and one of the key pillars of the plan (at the time of writing) is the target of no new non-electric cars by 2035, and no new CO_2 emitting lorries or buses from 2040. Certain police forces are actively evaluating hybrid and electric vehicles, targeting emissions reductions and to comply with increasing local low emission zones, for example, London's Ultra Low Emission Zone (ULEZ). Current challenges include delivering sufficient vehicle charging infrastructure at locations where it is needed, and only limited availability of non-fossil fuel options for larger or more specialist police vehicles.

In 2022, the motoring publication *Auto Express* sent Freedom of Information Act requests to the UK's forty-five territorial police forces, enquiring as to the number of electric vehicles in use and the number of available charging points. At that time, *Auto Express* reported that the Metropolitan Police had 264 electric vehicle charging points and a total of ninety-nine electric cars, vans and motorcycles (including the electric BMW i3, Nissan Leaf and e-NV200 van). Gloucestershire Constabulary ranked second, with a total of eighty-three vehicles and fifty-nine charging points. Across those who responded, Auto Express noted that the BMW i3, Nissan Leaf, Vauxhall Corsa-e and Nissan e-NV200 were the most popular electric vehicles. As an alternative to electric vehicles, the Metropolitan Police also operates a small fleet of hydrogen cell-powered Toyota Mirai cars.

Of particular note, the British Transport Police has declared its intention to operate an all-electric car fleet by 2025. In 2022, it announced a Tesla Model 3 had been introduced at its Guildford Police Station as its first electric response vehicle, one of eighty electric vehicles since purchased by the force. It introduced further electric response models the same year, two Kia EV6 and two Polestar 2 cars. For a response vehicle to be selected, it needed to deliver a 300-mile range and have fast charging to deliver 100 miles of range within ten minutes. Other electric cars within the BTP fleet include the Peugeot e-208 and Vauxhall Corsa-e.

Avon and Somerset Police operates several all-electric, zero-emission patrol cars including this 2020 Renault ZOE, WX20 ECT, seen in Bristol in May 2022.

British Transport Police 2022 Kia EV6 GT-Line OU22 CWR. With a range of over 300 miles between charges and zero carbon emissions, this supports the BTP's electric vehicle commitment. It was seen at Stratford station in East London in May 2024.

Increased Interoperability

To decrease costs and maximise vehicle utilisation, many police forces are exploring how to share vehicles and their functionality with neighbouring forces, and in some cases with fire and rescue or ambulance services. The Police Act of 1996 requires Police and Crime Commissioners and Chief Constables to constantly review where collaboration with other forces would increase efficiency and operational effectiveness: Sections 22 and 23 of the Act provide the legal framework which governs how collaborative services are to be delivered.

There are many examples of how neighbouring territorial police forces have joined together to deliver both specialist functions as well as administrative capabilities. One is the coming together of certain parts of Surrey Police and Sussex Police: operationally this has included Roads Policing Units, Tactical Firearms Units, police dog units and crime scene investigators, whose respective vehicles now carry both force crests. Behind the scenes, vehicle recovery, human resources, security vetting and insurance are examples of activities now provided centrally by the combined organisation.

Other collaborations are already in place, including the provision of air support from the National Police Air Service (NPAS) and the services of Regional Organised Crime Units (ROCUs). Other regional capabilities include marine and search services, for example, the North Western Police Underwater Search and Marine Unit (which provides marine policing, underwater search and confined space search from mid-Wales to the Scottish Borders) is a collaborative service for Cumbria Constabulary, Greater Manchester Police, Lancashire Constabulary, Merseyside Police and North Wales Police.

An example of collaboration with a fire service is Northamptonshire's Joint Operations/Command Unit: a 22-tonne 2016 Scania G320 lorry, which features satellite, digital and private communications, is deployed to major or complex incidents as well as large-scale community events. Jointly operated by Northamptonshire Police and Northamptonshire Fire and Rescue Service, it has downlink capabilities to view live video from police helicopters above, operates a surveillance drone and works closely with the Arson Task Force.

In 2019, Devon and Cornwall Police joined Cornwall Fire and Rescue Service and South Western Ambulance Service in introducing Tri-Service Safety Officers, focusing on engagement, early intervention and prevention activities. Their vehicles carry the Battenburg schemes of all three services. Skoda Octavia YP61 LJN is seen in Launceston.

Northamptonshire Police and Northamptonshire Fire and Rescue Service have a Joint Operations Unit, manned by both police and fire officers at major incidents or events. It is supported by this 2017 Volvo XC70 KX17 CAV, which can be used as a drone unit when required.

Glossary

ACPO	Association of Chief Police Officers
AFO	Authorised Firearms Officer
ANPR	Automatic Number Plate Recognition
ARV	Armed Response Vehicle
ASU	Air Support Unit
BCU	Basic Command Unit
BIAC	Belfast International Airport Constabulary
BTP	British Transport Police
CCS	Crown Commercial Service
CIU	Collision Investigation Unit
CMPG	Central Motorway Patrol Group (West Midlands Police and Staffordshire Police)
CNC	Civil Nuclear Constabulary (previously UKAEAC)
CTC	Chiltern Transport Consortium
DPG	Diplomatic Protection Group (SO16), Metropolitan Police
DTU	Driver Training Unit
ERU	Emergency Response Unit (London Underground)
GDP	Gibraltar Defence Police
IRV	Incident Response Vehicle
JCU	Joint Command Unit
JOU	Joint Operations Unit
LPU	Local Policing Unit
MDP	Ministry of Defence Police
MPU	Marine Policing Unit
NAPFM	National Association of Police Fleet Managers
NPT	Neighbourhood Policing Team
OCU	Operational Command Unit
OSU	Operational Support Unit
PAD	Passive Alert Detection (police dogs)
PaDP	Parliamentary and Diplomatic Protection, Metropolitan Police (previously DPG)
PSNI	Police Service of Northern Ireland (previously RUC)
PSU	Police Support Unit
PVI	Police Vehicle Incident
RAFP	Royal Air Force Police
RGP	Royal Gibraltar Police

RHIB	Rigid Hull Inflatable Boat
RIB	Rigid Inflatable Boat
RMP	Royal Military Police
RNP	Royal Navy Police
ROCU	Regional Organised Crime Units
RPC	Royal Parks Constabulary
RPU	Roads Policing Unit
RTC	Road Traffic Collision
RUC	Royal Ulster Constabulary (later PSNI)
SEG	Special Escort Group
SFO	Specialist Firearms Officer
TETRA	Terrestrial Trunked Radio
TFO	Tactical Flight Officer
TFU	Tactical Firearms Unit
TPAC	Tactical Pursuit and Containment
TVP	Thames Valley Police
UKAEAC	UK Atomic Energy Authority Constabulary (later CNC)
VASCAR	Visual Average Speed Computer and Recorder